ST. CHARLES COUNTY COMMUNITY COLLEGE

3 9835 00032595 5

W9-DIR-681

Where Our Children Play

Community Park Playground Equipment

Editors

DONNA THOMPSON

University of Northern Iowa

LOUIS BOWERS

University of South Florida

A Project Of The
AMERICAN ALLIANCE FOR HEALTH, PHYSICAL EDUCATION,
RECREATION AND DANCE
AMERICAN ASSOCIATION FOR LEISURE AND RECREATION
COMMITTEE ON PLAY

SCCCC - LIBRARY
4601 Mid Rivers Mall Drive
St. Peters, MO 63376

Copyright © 1989
AMERICAN ALLIANCE FOR HEALTH, PHYSICAL EDUCATION,
RECREATION AND DANCE
1900 ASSOCIATION DRIVE
RESTON, VA 22091

ISBN 0-88314-411-5

Purposes of the American Alliance For Health, Physical Education, Recreation and Dance

The American Alliance is an educational organization, structured for the purposes of supporting, encouraging, and providing assistance to member groups and their personnel throughout the nation as they seek to initiate, develop, and conduct programs in health, leisure, and movement-related activities for the enrichment of human life.

Alliance objectives include:

1. Professional growth and development—to support, encourage, and provide guidance in the development and conduct of programs in health, leisure, and movement-related activities which are based on the needs, interests, and inherent capacities of the individual in today's society.

2. Communication—to facilitate public and professional understanding and appreciation of the importance and value of health, leisure, and movement-related activities as they contribute toward human well-being.

3. Research—to encourage and facilitate research which will enrich the depth and scope of health, leisure, and movement-related activities; and to disseminate the findings to the profession and other interested and concerned publics.

4. Standards and guidelines—to further the continuous development and evaluation of standards within the profession for personnel and programs in health, leisure, and movement-related activities.

5. Public affairs—to coordinate and administer a planned program of professional, public, and governmental relations that will improve education in areas of health, leisure, and movement-related activities.

6. To conduct such other activities as shall be approved by the Board of Governors and the Alliance Assembly, provided that the Alliance shall not engage in any activity which would be inconsistent with the status of an educational and charitable organization as defined in Section 501(c)(3) of the Internal Revenue Code of 1954 or any successor provision thereto, and none of the said purposes shall at any time be deemed or construed to be purposes other than the public benefit purposes and objectives consistent with such educational and charitable status.

Bylaws, Article III

DEDICATION

Many dedicated professionals have contributed to this publication. Some have given a lifetime of work with the hope that the results will benefit children. That was the case with Dr. Eileen Warrell (1932-1988). She taught physical education for elementary students and physical education majors at Simon Fraser University in British Columbia, Canada. Eileen was active in her national physical education association, contributed to several books, including a chapter in *Play Spaces For Children*. She reached across the border to join our Committee On Play in planning and presenting material to several convention sessions. We appreciate her clear thinking and caring suggestions on behalf of children.

Eileen's efforts reflect the international concern about play structures for children. The editors wish to dedicate this book to the memory of Eileen Warrell and to her many contributions to the joyful play of children.

Correction

Please insert on p. vii.

Susan Hudson is an associate professor and program coordinator of recreation at the University of North Texas at Denton. She has expertise in facilities design, administration, and delivery of recreation programs and services.

ABOUT THE AUTHORS

Louis Bowers is a professor of Physical Education at the University of South Florida. He has been the principal person responsible for tabulating and describing the results of the Committee On Play's surveys for elementary school playgrounds and park play structures. He designs play structures, is a founding member of the Committee On Play, and writes widely regarding play structures.

Lawrence D. Bruya is a professor and head of the Department of Physical Education at Washington State University, Pullman. He has edited two volumes about elementary school playgrounds, served as chairperson for the Committee On Play, and consults regarding play structures.

Marcia Carter is an associate professor of Recreation at the University of Wisconsin-LaCrosse. She recently received the National Therapeutic Recreation Society's Prestigious Award for Distinguished Service and was elected to AALR's Board of Directors.

Annie Clement is a professor of Physical Education at Cleveland State University, Cleveland. As a lawyer, she holds the LLD Degree, has studied litigation regarding playgrounds and is a past NASPE President.

Mike Crawford is an associate professor of Recreation at the University of Missouri, Columbia. He is active in NRPA and IPA and has recently completed, with a colleague, a project about play structures.

Ralph Smith is an associate professor of Recreation at Penn State University, University Station. He is particularly concerned about accessibility of play equipment.

Donna Thompson is an associate professor of Physical Education at the University of Northern Iowa, Cedar Falls. She is chairperson of the Committee On Play, contributed to the volumes which reported information about school playgrounds, is secretary of the ASTM Task Force to develop standards for public use playgrounds, and consults regarding play structures.

Fran Wallach is president of Total Recreation Management Services Incorporated. She is a member of the Committee On Play, has consulted with national equipment companies, is chairperson of the ASTM Task Force to develop standards for public use playgrounds, and consults regarding maintenance programs and play structures.

A GUIDE TO FIGURES, ILLUSTRATIONS, PICTURES AND TABLES

CHAPTER	ITEM	CREDIT
1	Tables 1.1, 1.2 Figure 1.1	Bruya
4	Figure 4.1 4 Pictures	Bruya Carter
6	Figures 6.1, 6.2, 6.3	Bruya
7	Figure 7.3 2 Pictures	Wallach/Bruya Wallach
8	Figures 8.1, 8.2, 8.3	Bruya
9	Figures 9.1, 9.2, 9.3, 9.4, 9.5	Bruya

* Unless otherwise stated, the figures, illustrations, pictures, and tables were supplied by the author of each chapter.

CONTENTS

Dedication v

About the Authors vii

A Guide to Figures, Illustrations, Pictures and Tables ix

1. Introduction, *D. Thompson* 3

2. The National Survey of Community Park Playground Equipment,
   L. Bowers 9

3. Results of the Survey, *L. Bowers* 15

4. Location, Accessibility and Equipment on Park Playgrounds,
   S. Hudson 27

5. Swings, Slides, and Climbing Equipment,
   M. Crawford 37

6. Rotating, Spring Rocking and Seesaw Equipment, *M. Carter* 51

7. Sand Play Containers, Wading Pools, Signs, Trees,
   and Pathways, *F. Wallach* 61

8. Litigation and Playgrounds, *A. Clement* 73

9. Plan of Action: Reflections and Recommendations,
   R. Smith 85

APPENDICES 99

A. MISSION STATEMENT FOR THE COMMITTEE ON PLAY 101

B. TRAINED VOLUNTEER SURVEY ADMINISTRATORS 105

C. PLAYGROUND SELECTION PROCESS 109

D. NATIONAL PARK PLAYGROUND EQUIPMENT SURVEY
INSTRUMENT USED IN THE STUDY 113

WHERE OUR CHILDREN PLAY
COMMUNITY PARK PLAYGROUND EQUIPMENT

1

Introduction
by Donna Thompson

When you think of community park playgrounds, what images
come to your mind? Children respond by wondering whether or not
there is a merry-go-round to sit on, sand to dig in, a swing to climb or
swing on, or a place to play ball. Parenting adults are concerned about
the size of the equipment in relation to the age of the intended user,
proximity to home, whether or not the play area is secured by a fence,
the height of the equipment, and the surfacing placed on the ground
under each piece. Other adults whose professional lives deal with
recreation wonder whether or not appropriate equipment will accommodate the users in the area, be safe enough to prevent serious injury,
or reduce the likelihood of a lawsuit. Those kinds of images and more
guided the establishment of AALR's Committee On Play in 1981.

Background Connections:
The Committee On Play

The Committee On Play is a subdivision of the American Association for Leisure and Recreation whose parent group is The American
Alliance for Health, Physical Education, Recreation, and Dance. The
Committee On Play is a consortial body with linkages to the International Association for the Child's Right to Play (IPA), Association for
Childhood International (ACEI), and the National Association for the
Education of Young Children (NAEYC). Efforts are being made to
obtain representation from the National Recreation and Park Association (NRPA), Play For All, and Environmental Design and Research
Association (EDRA). The Committee On Play also invites representation from other organizations that are interested in studying play.

Play And Play Environments

The Committee developed five mission statements about play. (Table 1.1.) This project is concerned with one of those purposes: to determine the environmental conditions which support play. A series of goal statements was developed related to each mission statement. (Table 1.2.) This is one of three projects which begins to accomplish the first goal concerned with the environmental conditions which support play. Thus, the goal of evaluating playgrounds and suggesting improvements is beginning to be accomplished. This publication also contributes to the goal of producing, distributing, and presenting information on play and play environments.

This book is the second in a series of projects undertaken by the Committee On Play in order to identify the existing environmental conditions which support play. A national survey of elementary school playgrounds was conducted in 1985-86. The results of that effort are available in two volumes: *Where Our Children Play: Elementary School Playground Equipment*, and *Play Spaces For Children* which were both published by AAHPERD in 1988. The data for the park playground project was collected in 1987-88. During 1988-89, the data from the daycare and preschool playgrounds is being collected. It is anticipated that a third volume will be written to convey the results about that phase of playground research.

Community Parks

The parks that were surveyed in this project were community parks. Although it is important to observe national parks, county parks, and private parks, it was decided that it would be more appropriate to deal with one type of park playground rather than compare equip-

---

Table 1.1. The AAHPERD—AALR:COP mission statement was approved by concensus of the Committee On Play constituency in 1983

COP Mission Statement

The committee shall:
- Investigate the role of play in American society and human culture;
- Work to understand the role of play in the physiological and psychological development of individuals;
- Determine the environmental conditions which support play;
- Distribute information about play;
- Advocate for the rights of children to play.

Table 1.2. The AAHPERD—AALR:COP goal statements were accepted in 1983 by the constituency of the Committee On Play

Goal Statements for COP

Role of Play
1. in development and learning
2. as a social force
3. as a therapeutic tool

Ramifications of Play
1. processing and organizing information
2. improving affective, cognitive, and psychomotor functioning

Environmental Conditions Supporting Play
1. evaluating playgrounds and suggesting improvements
2. determining design criteria for playgrounds
3. determining function and purpose of play equipment
4. determine the use of durable, economical, and safe materials

Communication and Advocacy for Play
1. producing, distributing and presenting information on play
2. actively promoting play

ment in all types of park play environments. The instrument that was used in the survey would also be appropriate to survey the other types of park environments.

Writers

The editors of this book have been involved with the Committee On Play since its inception, and both were involved in the national elementary school playground project. Bowers designed the instrument for both projects, Thompson is chair of the Committee On Play, and both authored chapters in the AAHPERD publications: *Where Our Children Play: Elementary School Playground Equipment,* and *Play Spaces For Children.* In addition, one of the other authors is a physical education specialist with a law degree, and the remaining authors are recreation specialists. Each author has a specific interest in playgrounds and a particular expertise to lend.

Readers

There are several groups of people who should be concerned with the results of this survey: the parents of children; professionals, including recreation specialists, park administrators, and board members who are responsible for playgrounds and children's play;

Figure 1.1. The people most likely to influence change and ultimately change the play structures on which children play.

and those who manufacture and design playground equipment. Lawyers may also find the information useful.

Readers will want to notice Bowers' description of the survey in Chapter 2 and his report on the over-all results in Chapter 3. Hudson raises some concerns about accessibility in Chapter 4. In Chapter 5, Crawford questions safety in relation to swings, slides, and climbing equipment. Carter, in Chapter 6, describes some benefits to children who may participate on rotating equipment. In Chapter 7, Wallach notes the importance of maintenance procedures in relation to sand and water play, trees, signs, and pathways. Clement reinforces the need for risk management procedures in Chapter 8, and finally, Smith makes four strong recommendations for change in relation to playground equipment or structures in Chapter 9.

Beneficiaries

Hopefully, children will be the real beneficiaries of the combined efforts of those who planned the project, those who gathered data, and those who have analyzed the findings and made suggestions for change. Each of the groups may influence changes in a different but significant manner (Figure 1.1).

Parents can use the information to influence licensing procedures based on safety, and to insist that maintenance procedures be established. This report gives some guidelines for safety and an instrument to gather such information.

Recreators should take note of the cautions that are raised regarding safety of play equipment. Board members may want to establish policies about safety on playgrounds, and address maintenance procedures for equipment. The survey also compares play theories and playground equipment, and the results may suggest that changes are in order, either in theory applied or in the type of equipment that children should use in order to stimulate play.

Lawyers will find some norms established and some recommendations for safety procedures. Manufacturers may need to pay attention to the observations regarding the safety of equipment, while maintenance procedures are addressed specifically for recreation specialists.

Purpose

The purpose of this publication is to describe the type and condition of playground equipment in community parks in the United States, and to indicate the current status and safety of that environment. The results are then compared to play theories to explore the ways the environment stimulates play. Lastly, appropriate suggestions for change are made for the reader to consider.

Challenge

The Committee On Play and the editors challenge the readers of this publication to help make playground equipment safer and more appropriate for the play of children.

2

National Survey of Community Park Playground Equipment

by Louis Bowers

In 1986, the Committee on Play of the American Association for Leisure and Recreation, an association of the American Alliance for Health, Physical Education, Recreation, and Dance initiated a survey of playground equipment available for use by children in community parks in the United States. The study was an extension of the 1985 National Survey of Elementary School Playground Equipment conducted by the AAHPERD Committee on Play. Both the 1985 and 1986 studies were conducted in order to secure accurate information which might be used by educators and designers to improve existing and future playground equipment in schools and community parks.

Survey Instrument Development

The Committee on Play made the decision to use the written survey instrument used in the 1985 National Survey of Elementary School Playground Equipment. This instrument had been formulated by Dr. Louis Bowers with review input by members of the Committee on Play. Field trials were also conducted at the University of South Florida by undergraduate physical education majors trained to administer the survey. Students reported in writing any problems encountered in using the survey on elementary school playgrounds in the Tampa, Florida area. This information was utilized in the final revision of the playground equipment survey.

The total process of constructing the survey instrument, review of the instrument by a panel of experts, conducting field trials, and making final revisions of the survey instrument took place between May 1984 and April 1985. Upon completion of this process, the survey instrument was named the AAHPERD-AALR-COP National Elementary School Playground Equipment Survey.

The six-page survey instrument was designed to secure information regarding: 1) the type and the quantity of play structures, 2) location of each play structure on the playground, 3) the maintenance status of each play structure, 4) the height and configuration of each play structure, and 5) the type of surface material under each play structure. In addition, the survey provides information regarding broken or missing parts, sharp edges and projections, small openings within the structures, and other safety conditions.

The survey instruments consisted of 12 sections with a minimum of 4 and a maximum of 10 items in each section for a total of 100 items.

Sixty three of the items call for a yes (✓) or no (X) response, whereas, 37 involved a quantitative response. The items were designed to provide objective reporting of the type, size, location, or condition of the play structures while not necessitating that the surveyor make judgments regarding the safe or unsafe conditions of the equipment. Based on observations of 1,745 different play structures, data obtained by the 100-item survey will be reported later in this publication. The categories of play structures which were used identified 430 climbing structures, 398 swing structures, 378 slide structures, 70 seesaws, 97 rotating structures, 30 designated sand play areas, 192 rocking structures, and 6 water play areas.

All equipment under each of the categories was assessed as a group. Consequently, although one, two, or more structures of a particular category might be present on a playground, if one structure had a

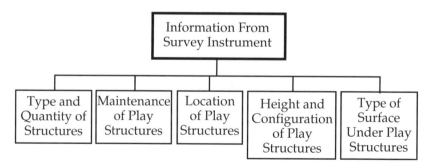

Figure 2.1. The survey instrument was designed to provide information in the five above areas.

broken part or sharp edge, the condition was reported to exist for that category of equipment on the playground. If more than one structure was found to have the same above condition, it was reported to exist only once for the category. This reporting procedure was based on the premise that each of the play structures within a category is available for play by children, thus, if any one piece of equipment is poorly constructed or not maintained, it constitutes a problem in using that type of equipment on that playground. Measurements of height, distances between parts, and diameter of handholds are made and reported on for each play structure.

In order to minimize distractions, the survey instrument was designed to assess play structures without children playing on them. Using this approach eliminated questions related to the amount of play which occurs on certain types of equipment or the various ways children play on different play structures.

The items on the survey provide information which allows the Committee on Play members and others to compare the findings of the study with local standards for play structures or to recommended guidelines of the Consumer Product Safety Commission (CPSC, 1978a; CPSC, 1978b; CPSC, 1979; CPSC, 1982a; CPSC, 1982b).

The survey instrument developed for the study is available for future assessments of playgrounds and the results may be used in analyzing needed improvements in play structures.

The survey instrument was designed to be administered within 30 minutes on each playground site. The average amount of time needed to administer the survey in the National Survey of Community Park Playground Equipment was 26 minutes.

Reliability of Survey Instrument

Forty-four volunteer participants (See Appendix B) from 36 states received training in the administration of the survey at the 1985 AAHPERD National Convention in Atlanta. The two-hour training session included a 35-mm slide presentation of examples of all assessment items on the survey. Following the training session, the volunteers used the survey instrument to independently assess playground equipment in Candler Park in Atlanta. The percentage of agreement between participants on each item of the survey was computed for the 44 independent surveys, and involved dividing the number of most frequent responses for each item by the total number of responses and multiplying by 100.

For example, if 40 of 44 surveyors checked "yes" for a survey item, the inter-rater agreement for that item was 90.9 percent. For those survey items which called for quantitative recordings such as "how many," or "how high," the percentage of responses which were exactly alike were computed.

Section	No.		Percentage
1.	Location and Accessibility		80.8
2.	Placement and Size of Equipment		69.8
3.	Type and Numbers of Equipment		75.6
4.	Swinging Equipment		85.7
5.	Sliding Equipment		76.6
6.	Climbing Equipment		63.7
9.	Seesaws		81.0
12.	Signs, Trees, Pathways		81.1

Figure 2.2 . Percentages of inter-rater exact agreement for sections of the survey instrument.

The percentage of inter-rater agreement among the 44 trained volunteers was also computed for all the items on the survey. The inter-rater agreement percentage for the entire survey was 80.1 percent. This compared favorably to the a priori criterion level of 80 percent exact agreement reported by Roberton & DiRicco, 1981. Sections 7, 8, 10, and 11 of the survey instrument were omitted from the inter-rater agreement computation since rotating and rocking equipment and designated sand play areas and wading pools were not found in Candler Park. Figure 2.2 shows the Inter-Rater Exact Agreement for Sections of the Survey Instrument.

Written comments made on the survey instruments by the trained volunteers were utilized to record several items on the survey. This revised survey, which was named the AAHPERD-AALR-COP Playground Equipment Survey was used in the 1985 National Survey of Elementary School Playgrounds and in the 1987 National Survey of Community Park Playground Equipment being reported in this publication. A copy of this survey is included as Appendix D.

Compilation of Project Data

A total of 198 playground surveys administered by 40 trained volunteers were sent to Dr. Louis Bowers at the University of South Florida and tabulated under Dr. Bowers' supervision by Ms. Karen Jacobs and Ms. Amy Russell, both graduate research assistants. Dr. Bowers checked data tabulations and computed the percentages of "Yes" and "No" responses and the mean scores of the quantitative response items.

The results of the 198 surveys representing parks in 23 states were presented at the 1987 AAHPERD Convention and shared with members of the Committee on Play, and were further shared with the authors selected to write the chapters of this publication.

**NATIONAL SURVEY OF COMMUNITY PARK
PLAYGROUND EQUIPMENT**

Figure 2.3. A map of the United States of America which indicates the states in which the surveys were administered.

The distribution of the number of playgrounds surveyed within the United States is shown in Figure 2.3. Appendix C describes the park selection process.

Bibliography

Bowers, L. (1976). Toward a Science of Playground Design. *Journal of Health, Physical Education and Recreation, 50(6),* 51-54.

Bowers, L. (1981, November). Review of Consumer Product Safety Commission Standards for Playgrounds. *Journal of Health, Physical Education, Recreation and Dance.*

Roberton, M.A., & DiRicco, R. (1981). Motor skill sequence for mentally retarded children. *American Corrective Therapy Journal, (55),* 148-154.

U.S. Consumer Product Safety Commission: Division of Human Factors (1978a). *Human factors analysis of injuries associated with public playground equipment.* Washington, D.C.: Government Printing Office.

U.S. Consumer Product Safety Commission (1978b). *Play Happy, Play Safe, playground equipment guide.* Washington, D.C.: Government Printing Office.

U.S. Consumer Product Safety Commission: Bureau of Epidemiology (1979). *Hazard analysis of playground equipment.* Washington, D.C.: Government Printing Office.

U.S. Consumer Product Safety Commission (1982a). *A handbook for public playground safety, (Volume I: General guidelines for new and existing playgrounds).* Washington, D.C.: Government Printing Office.

U.S. Consumer Product Safety Commission (1982b). *A handbook for public playground safety, (Volume II: Technical guidelines for equipment and surfacing).* Washington, D.C.: Government Printing Office.

3

Results of the Survey
by Louis Bowers

The results of the National Survey of Playground Equipment in Community Parks, presented in the following series of 21 tables, are based on assessments of 198 community parks located in 18 states. The surveys were administered by 40 volunteer professional recreators and physical educators. The playgrounds surveyed were located in community parks which were randomly selected from a list of all parks located in each of the park districts included in the study. A total of 1,745 play structures were surveyed in 198 parks. Ten of the community parks included in the sample did not have any playground equipment. The average amount of time used to administer the survey in each park was 26 minutes.

The results of the 198 surveys which are reported in this chapter were compiled at the University of South Florida by graduate assistants Karen Jacobs and Amy Russell under the direction of Dr. Louis Bowers.

Section One focuses on the security of the play area and accessibility up to and on the play equipment. (See Figure 3.1.)

Section Two records the placement, size of play equipment for younger children, and exposed concrete footings. (See Figure 3.2.)

Section Three quantifies the types of play equipment found in the community parks surveyed. (See Figure 3.3.)

Sections Four through Twelve of the survey instruments report on the size, physical structure, condition, and ground covering beneath individual types of equipment. The play equipment was categorized as swinging, sliding, climbing, rotating, rocking, seesaws, sand play, or wading pool type equipment.

Survey Section 1: Location and Accessibility of Playground Equipment		
Item	% yes	% no
1.1 easily viewed	83	13
1.2 three foot wall	25	75
1.3 wheelchair access to equipment	16	84
1.4 wheelchair access on equipment	14	86

Figure 3.1. Results of Data Compilation for Section One

Survey Section 2: Placement and Size of Playground Equipment		
Item	% yes	% no
2.1 ten foot space between equipment	75	25
2.2 traffic patterns on designated pathways	81	19
2.3 smaller equipment for younger children	75	25
2.4 large and small equipment separated	43	57
2.5 exposed concrete footings	1.8 per playground	

Figure 3.2. Results of Data Compilation for Section Two

Survey Section 3: Types and Numbers of Equipment

Equipment	total no. present	ave. per playground	% total playground equipment
swing structures	370	1.86	21.2
flat slides	308	1.55	17.5
spring rockers	192	.97	11
merry-go-round	97	.49	5.5
fireman pole	95	.48	5.4
overhead ladders	92	.46	5.3
chinning bars	91	.45	5.2
seesaws	70	.35	4
monkey bars	66	.33	3.8
balance beams	64	.32	3.6
suspended bridge	55	.27	3.2
tube slides	55	.27	3.2
geodesic dome climber	41	.21	2.4
parallel bars	41	.21	2.3
sand play containers	30	.15	1.7
exer-glides	24	.12	1.4
concrete tunnels	20	.10	1.14
spiral slides	15	.07	.86
water play containers	6	.03	.34
animal figures	5	.03	.28
overhead rings	4	.02	.229
tire swings	4	.02	.229
Total pieces of equipment	1,745	8.8	99.59

Figure 3.3. Results of Data Compilation for Section Three

Survey Section 4: Swing Equipment, Descriptive Information Based on 398 Swing Structures				
Item	number	total	percent	misc.
4.1 # swing seats	7/plgrd			
4.2 # metal/wood seats		328	26%	
4.3 #swivel seats		131	16%	
4.12 Distance between seats				26 inches
From a total of 1,262 available swing seats				

Figure 3.4a - Partial Results of Data Compilation for Section Four

Survey Section 4: Percentages for Swinging Equipment		
Item	% yes	% no
4.5 swings for young children	59	41
4.6 separate young children swing structure	45	55
4.7 swing barriers	11	89
4.8 structures firmly anchored	98	2
4.9 sharp edges, projections	25	75
4.10 moving parts in good repair	73	27
4.11 chain covered	20	80

Figure 3.4b - Partial Results of Data Compilation for Section Four

Survey Section 4: Surfacing Materials Found Under the Swings	
Material	% material
asphalt	3
clay	9
concrete	1
grass	12
mulch	9
pea gravel	10
rubber matting	.5
sand	40
other	15.5

Figure 3.4c - Partial Results of Data Compilation for Section Four

Survey Section 5: Percentages for 378 Pieces of Sliding Equipment		
Item	% yes	% no
5.1 broken equipment	8	92
5.2 sharp edges, protrusions	16	84
5.3 structures firmly anchored	92	8
5.4 wide slide	28	72
5.5 safe sliding surface	93	7
5.6 deceleration chute	80	20
5.7 above 13" high slide exit	47	53
5.9 guard rail on platform	89	11

Figure 3.5a - Partial Results of Data Compilation for Section Five

Survey Section 5: Percentages for Sliding Equipment Height, Based on Item 5.8 for 378 Pieces	
Height	% slide structures
under 8 feet	68
8 feet - 9 feet 11.9 inches	18
10 feet - 10 feet 11.9 inches	6
11 feet - up	8

Figure 3.5b - Partial Results of Data Compilation for Section Five

Survey Section 5: Surface Materials Found Under 378 Pieces of Sliding Equipment	
Material	% material
asphalt	.5
clay	8
concrete	1
grass	11
mulch	9
pea gravel	11
rubber matting	1.5
sand	44
other	14.5

Figure 3.5c - Partial Results of Data Compilation for Section Five

Survey Section 6: Percentages for 426 Pieces of Climbing Equipment		
Item	% yes	% no
6.1 securely fastened parts	92	8
6.2 firmly anchored structures	99	1
6.3 finger traps in pipes	19	81
6.5 sharp edges, protrusions	13	87
6.7 V angle entrapment	14	86
6.4 hand hold diameter	2.53 inches	
6.6 average distance between levels	19.60 inches	

Figure 3.6a - Partial Results of Data Compilation for Section Six

Survey Section 6: Percentages for Climbing Equipment Height, Based on Item 6.8 for 426 Pieces	
Height	% climbing structures
9 feet	82
10 feet	10
12 feet	3
13 feet	1
15 feet	4
average maximum height for climbing equipment mentioned above = 7.4 feet	

Figure 3.6b - Partial Results of Data Compilation for Section Six

**Survey Section 6: Surface Materials Found Under
426 Pieces of Climbing Equipment with an
Average Maximum Height of 7.4 Feet**

Material	% of Material
asphalt	2
clay	2
concrete	2
grass	21
mulch	9
pea gravel	7
rubber matting	1
sand	43
other	13

Figure 3.6c - Partial Results of Data Compilation for Section Six

**Survey Section 7: Percentages for 97 Pieces of
Rotating Equipment**

	Item	% yes	% no
7.1	firmly anchored structures	96	4
7.2	securely fastened parts	94	6
7.3	sharp edges, protrusions	28	72
7.4	rotation-post area open	46	54
7.5	perimeter clearing of 20 feet	32	68

Figure 3.7a - Partial Results of Data Compilation for Section
Seven

Survey Section 7: Surface Materials Found Under 97 Pieces of Rotating Equipment	
Material	% of Material
asphalt	5
clay	9
concrete	1
grass	10
mulch	9
pea gravel	14
rubber matting	0
sand	42
other	10

Figure 3.7b - Partial Results of Data Compilation for Section Seven

Survey Section 8: Percentages for 192 Pieces of Rocking Equipment		
Item	% yes	% no
8.1 firmly anchored structures	91	9
8.2 all parts are present	78	22
8.3 all parts are securely fastened	83	17
8.4 sharp edges, protrusion	41	59
8.5 seating less than 30 inches from the ground	93	7
8.6 3 inch long hand hold	76	24
8.7 4 x 6 inch foot rest	78	22
8.8 spring action pinches possible	37	63

Figure 3.8a - Partial Results of Data Compilation for Section Eight

Survey Section 8: Surface Materials Found Under 33 Pieces of Rocking Equipment	
Material	% of Material
asphalt	0
clay	9
concrete	5
grass	10
mulch	3
pea gravel	13
rubber matting	0
sand	46
other	14

Figure 3.8b - Partial Results of Data Compilation for Section Eight

Survey Section 9: Percentages for 70 Pieces of Seesaw Equipment		
Item	% yes	% no
9.1 firmly anchored structures	98	2
9.2 all parts are securely fastened	71	29
9.3 sharp edges, protrusion	35	65
9.5 3 inch double hand holds	79	21
9.6 body can pass beneath while it's in action	57	43
9.7 cushioned ground strike	17	83
9.8 accessible pivotal moving parts	60	40
9.4 seating height - average at the highest point 3.8 feet		

Figure 3.9a - Partial Results of Data Compilation for Section Nine

Survey Section 9: Surface Materials Found Under 70 Pieces of Seesaw Equipment

Material	% of Material
asphalt	4
clay	2
concrete	0
grass	20
mulch	9
pea gravel	16
rubber matting	0
sand	33
others	16

Figure 3.9b - Partial Results of Data Compilation for Section Nine

Survey Section 10: Percentages for 30 Designated Sand Play Areas

Item	% yes	% no
10.1 clean and free of debris	59	41
10.2 good drainage apparent	55	45
10.3 covered or located to exclude animals	19	81
10.4 adult seating available	75	25

Figure 3.10 - Partial Results of Data Compilation for Section Ten

Survey Section 11: Percentages for 6 Wading Pools

Item	% yes	% no
11.1 fenced and gated	53	47
11.2 clear and free of debris	79	21
11.4 adult seating provided	71	29

11.3 Filled water - average depth   15.5 inches

Figure 3.11 - Partial Results of Data Compilation for Section Eleven

Survey Section 12: Percentages for 198 Playgrounds with Signs, Trees, and Pathways		
Item	% yes	% no
12.1 signs which give help	2	98
12.2 signs which suggest restricted or limited use	11	89
12.3 signs which prohibit animals	13	87
12.5 shade available from structures	44	56
12.6 hard surfaces which could be used for wheel toys	44	56
12.4 average per playground	14 trees	

Figure 3.12 - Partial Results of Data Compilation for Section Twelve

The survey instrument used in the National Survey of Community Park Playground Equipment was designed to gather information regarding the location, number, size, condition, and ground covering under various types of playground equipment. The playgrounds were surveyed when children were not playing on the equipment so that use of the equipment would not affect data collection.

The next several chapters will focus on further analysis of the results in relation to the theories of play and safety aspects of the known ways in which children engage in play.

4

Location, Accessibility and Equipment on Park Playgrounds
by Susan Hudson

The organized public recreation movement in the United States started with the creation of playgrounds. In 1885, Dr. Marie Zakrewska wrote to the Massachusetts Emergency and Hygiene Association about the benefits that German children received from the "sand gardens" provided for their play and recreation. The members of the Association, enthused by the report, promptly placed a sand pile at the Parmenter Chapel for the recreational use of small children in the area (Kraus, 1984). From this humble beginning of the Boston Sand Garden, a national effort was soon launched to provide public play space for all children in the United States.

However, these early play spaces were designed more by the vision of the early recreation pioneers than by a solid understanding about design, safety, or play theories. An example of this early unscientific philosophy can be seen from the following resolution adopted at the first meeting of the Playground Association of America in 1906:

> That while there is no inherent relation between space and children, and the exact amount of space required cannot be determined, it is our belief that the present London requirement of 30 sq. ft. of playground for each child of the school is the minimum with which the proper amount of light, air and space for play and gymnastics can be secured. (Gold, 1973, p. 144)

Unfortunately, until recently, most standards for playgrounds have remained as general as the above example. At the same time, playground apparatus has become much more sophisticated, both in size, shape, and overall design. Thus, the question that faces that profession today is, "Do our community playgrounds reflect the play values and standards of the 1980s or are they still a reflection of their 'sand garden' origins?"

This chapter will consider the results of the National Project for the Assessment of Community Park Playgrounds, implications for the recreation profession regarding the safety and design of community playgrounds, and ways the present day playgrounds contribute to the play development of children.

Location and Accessibility

In 1980, the United States Consumer Product Safety Commission published guidelines for playgrounds and play equipment that included considerations for location and accessibility of equipment (USCPSC, 1980). In terms of location of the overall playground site, USCPSC recommended that playground designers keep the site free from visual barriers that could hamper supervision. This is especially important in order to prevent children from being kidnapped or molested. The park playgrounds in the national study have adhered well to this USCPSC guideline. Eighty-three percent (83%) of the playgrounds were located at sites that were easily viewed by parents, supervisors, and children.

Although this guideline makes sense in terms of ease of supervision, it does have some other implications. In 1988, homeowners in a suburb of Dallas, Texas complained to the park board that a proposed playground did not blend into the surrounding environment. While they realized the need to have the playground in an accessible and visible place in the neighborhood park, they objected to the bright colors (red, yellow, orange and green) of the equipment. "Mute it or move it" was their cry. On the other end of the controversy are the play theorists, such as Michael Ellis, who see in the bright colors a stimuli that impact upon the individual to produce a high arousal potential (Ellis, 1973). Thus, visibility is an important safety as well as play development standard. At the same time it may have some other implications for the community that extend beyond the playground parameters.

A second site recommendation by the USCPSC was that a playground area be surrounded by some type of barrier to "keep children within the grounds and prevent them from running into the street." (USCPSC, 1980, p. 5). It should be noted though that barricades work both ways. A fence or hedge in a multi-use park can serve to prevent stray balls, running children and other unwanted items from freely entering into the play space and causing an unwanted hazard. Thus, some type of "experience buffer" for playgrounds would seem to be of utmost importance in the design of these play spaces (see Figure 41.). Unfortunately, only 25 percent of the playgrounds in the survey provided some type of buffer to separate the play spaces from the other activities occurring around these areas.

Since the early 1970s, professionals have slowly become aware that not all children are able to walk into playgrounds. Yet despite inroads in legislation and awareness programs, accessibility for children with disabling conditions appears to be almost nonexistent in public playgrounds. Only 16 percent of the playgrounds in the survey provided wheelchair access to equipment and only 14 percent of the playgrounds in the study had apparatus that allowed wheelchairs on the equipment. Clearly, this is a glaring weakness in the design of our nation's community playgrounds.

Placement and Size

The placement and size of playground equipment impact the play experience of children in several ways. The first obvious way has to do with safety.

A safety zone should surround each piece of equipment. That is the space which will allow the child to swing out in a swing, slide and

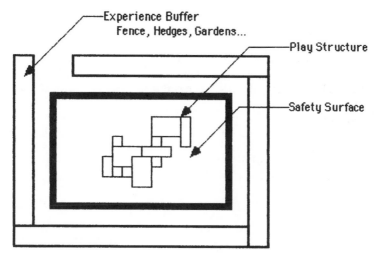

Figure 4.1. The 'Experience Buffer' can serve to control entrance and exit to the play structure so that unwanted interferences are limited.

jump off the end of a slide, or manipulate a piece of apparatus without endangering anyone in the surrounding area. The USCPSC recommends that at least eight feet separate estimate use zones of equipment. The National Survey of Community Playgrounds found that 75 percent of the community playgrounds surveyed had at least ten feet of space between equipment. While this high statistic is encouraging for the safety of our children, it should be 100 percent.

In addition, special attention must be paid to the traffic flow around equipment. Of particular concern would be pathways that move children in front of slides, swings and other equipment where children are moving on and off. Again, the community playgrounds seemed to meet this standard well since 81 percent of the playgrounds surveyed had attempted to move traffic on designated pathways.

An important safety concern is the placement of play apparatus to create flow from one play experience to another. A playground that is designed to emphasize exploration and investigation is much more conducive to arousal-seeking elements of children's play. This type of play space can be provided with the proper placement of apparatus which allows the children choices and opportunities to make decisions as they flow from one piece of equipment to another. Although the evidence of "play flow" was not an element of this study, it should be an important consideration in the placement of any playground equipment.

Providing the appropriately sized equipment for the playground is also a critical consideration from both a safety and play theory standpoint. Children need to be able to test their skills on equipment that is made for their size and physical development.

Seventy-five percent (75%) of the playgrounds in the National Survey did have smaller equipment for younger children. Although this is an encouraging statistic, it is somewhat diminished by the fact that a majority of the playgrounds, 57 percent, did not separate large and small equipment on the playground. Thus, children in exercising their free choice, may play on equipment that is too complex for their abilities.

Playground equipment for younger and older children needs to be separate, according to play theory, as well as from a safety point of view. According to Ellis' arousal-seeking theory of play:

1. Children engage in play for the stimulation that they receive.

2. That stimulation must contain elements of uncertainty.

3. The interactions producing the stimulation must rise in complexity with the accumulation of knowledge about or experience with an object. (Ellis, 1973, p. 135)

Viewed in this light, small slides and swings appropriate to age group would allow children to explore the world in an environment that is not overwhelming. As children become familiar with that world, variations of the apparatus (height, size, complexity) would provide the novelty needed to sustain the play experience.

Separation of these play experiences can be achieved through the proper placement of equipment which directs children into either the more complex equipment or to small equipment that may be more appropriate for the age group. Unfortunately, this element is not clearly defined in the survey. It is assumed that the majority of the playgrounds in the survey mixed small equipment with large equipment with no physical or design barrier between the two.

The final concern about equipment placement addressed in the survey involved exposed concrete footings of apparatus. Although it is imperative from a safety point of view to firmly anchor various pieces of equipment, these anchors may become a safety factor as they gradually become exposed through normal wear and tear. It appears that most community playgrounds have done a good job in maintenance since so few were exposed (an average of 1.8 per playground were recorded).   Even though one would hope for a zero average on this particular item, the low score would indicate that quite a few playgrounds had no exposed footings.

Type and Numbers of Equipment

Although discussion concerning specific equipment will be the focus of subsequent chapters, an observation about the provision of overall playground apparatus will be covered in this section. Figure 3.3 (p. 17) presents a summary of the number and types of playground equipment found on the community playgrounds in the study.

It is apparent from viewing Figure 3.3, that the three most frequently found types of apparatus are climbing structures, swings, and slides, which altogether account for 63 percent of all the playground equipment reported. The majority of the remaining structures were spring rockers, merry-go-rounds, and seesaws which tend to move children on the equipment.

These survey results only confirm what Michael Ellis rather harshly stated when he called the average traditional playground a travesty (Ellis, 1973). According to Ellis, playgrounds are often abandoned by children because they fail to provide the arousal-seeking experiences that are at the core of children's play. Slides, swings, and monkey bars are not items that the child can manipulate to provide additional stimuli, nor do they in and of themselves offer increasing complexity of environment as the child revisits a playground. In short, most community playgrounds are boring.

If community playgrounds are to move beyond the "sand garden" mentality, recreation professionals need to provide, through the proper design and placement of equipment, a play environment that is arranged to emphasize exploration, investigation, and complexity of a child's world. Unfortunately the type of equipment described in this study, although somewhat safe in accessibility and placement, fails to provide a stimulating environment. Until designers understand that safety does not mean sterile environments, and that use of play theories can contribute to the overall goals of playground development, community play areas will be a reflection of their past rather than a vision of the future.

Conclusion

The results of the National Survey of Community Playgrounds provide both positive and negative reviews for the recreation profession. On the positive side, the survey indicates that the recreation profession has done a good job in providing play equipment that is visible for supervision, that has proper spacing between apparatus for safety, that shows a conscious effort to provide good traffic flow, and that makes some provision for different age groups.

On the negative side, however, the recreation profession receives low marks for providing playgrounds that are not accessible to children with disabling conditions, that do not separate large and small equipment, and, perhaps most damaging of all, apparatus that do not contribute to the overall play development of a child. The pictures within this chapter illustrate ways to make equipment more accessible.

As seen in the survey (Figure 3.3), park playgrounds still emphasize stationary apparatus that focus on the gross motor development of a child. This type of equipment would be appropriate if the "surplus energy of play" theory was still valid.

A ramp with handrails makes the merry-go-round accessible to those confined to wheelchairs and to those with braces, on crutches, or those who can crawl.

However, present day play theories such as developmental, learning, and arousal-seeking, would suggest that children's play is more than the expenditure of excess energy. Rather, these theories all point to children's intellectual as well as physical growth in the play experience. Thus, these theories indicate a need for play apparatus which encourages children to explore and interact with their environment. Clearly, equipment sunk in concrete which has no manipulative parts and which provides little opportunity to exercise free choice does not promote children's overall play experiences.

In short, the National Project for the Assessment of Community Park Playgrounds has shown that present day playgrounds reflect yesterday's, not today's, play theories. Perhaps that is one of the biggest contributions that this project has made to the parks and recreation field.

Only when contemporary park and recreation planners incorporate the modern ideas of arousal-seeking, exploration, and complexity in their designs, will playgrounds reflect the present and not the past. By pointing out this need, the National Project of the Assessment for Community Park Playgrounds has made a positive contribution from a negative finding. Hopefully, the profession and the children that the profession serves will benefit.

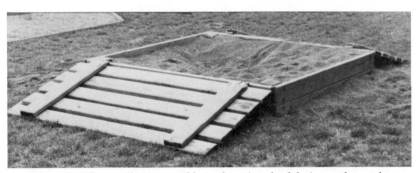

A ramp makes the sandbox accessible to those in wheelchairs or those who can crawl. A smooth ramp is another option.

A bench swing can be adjusted for those who need support or need to be confined by adding an additional side that swings down in order to allow access. It is still usable for others, as well. However, one might be concerned about the wood hanging down which might hit children if they fell out of the swing. The additional side should be attached in the upward position when not in use.

Bibliography

Bruya, L.D. and Langendorfer, S. J. (1988). *Where our children play, Vol. 1.* Reston, VA: AAHPERD.

Ellis, Michael. (1973). *Why People Play.* Princeton, NJ: Prentice Hall Inc.

Fein, G. (1979). Play in the acquisition of symbols. In L. Katz (Ed.), *Current topics in early childhood education.* Norwood, NJ: Ablex.

Frost, J. L. (1986). Children's playgrounds: Research and practice. In G. Fien (Ed), *Play.* Washington, D.C.: National Association for the Education of Young Children.

Gold, Seymour. (1973). *Urban Recreation Planning.* Philadelphia: Lea and Febiger.

Kraus, Richard. (1984). *Recreation and Leisure in Modern Society.* (3rd. Ed.). Glenview, IL: Scott, Foresman and Company.

Piaget, J. (1962). *Play, dreams and imitation in childhood.* New York: W. W. Norton.

Rubin, K. H., Maioni, T. L., & Hornung, M. (1976). Free play behaviors in middle- and lower-class preschoolers: Parten and Piaget revisited. *Child Development, 47,* 414-419.

Smilanski, S. (1968). *The effects of sociodramatic play on disadvantaged preschool children.* New York: John Wiley.

Sutton-Smith, B. (1967). The role of play in child development, *Young Children, 22,* 361-370.

U.S. Consumer Product Safety Commission. (1980a). *A handbook for public playground safety: Vol. I, General guidelines for new and existing playgrounds.* Washington, D.C.: U.S. Government Printing Office.

U.S. Consumer Product Safety Commission. (1980a). *A handbook for public playground safety: Vol. II. Technical guidelines for equipment and surfacing.* Washington, D.C.: U.S. Government Printing Office.

Wortham, S. (1988). Location, Accessibility and Equipment on Playgrounds. In L. D. Bruya & S. J. Langendorfer (Eds.), *Where our children play, Vol. 1.* Reston, VA: AAHPERD.

A swing can be made accessible for those confined in wheelchairs with a ramp that can be raised, lowered, and hooked to the chains.

5

Swings, Slides, and Climbing Equipment
by Michael Crawford

The cluster of outdoor challenge equipment reviewed in this chapter represents collectively the majority (83%) of playground equipment found in the National Survey of Community Parks (climber = 24%, swings = 23%, and slides = 12%), as well as being responsible for the majority (81%) of serious injuries (climber = 42%, swings = 23%, and slides = 16%) (USCPSC, 1980a). Additionally, the available research on play and traffic patterns supports information that in free play situations, aside from running and object play, behaviors on these apparatus are the most frequently engaged in (Van Alstyne, 1932; Wade, 1968; Brown, 1978; Gabbard and LeBlanc, 1980). Further, we know that this engagement is relatively universal across types of children, with gender, race, and socioeconomic backgrounds exerting almost no influence in the selection of playground behaviors while on play equipment (Eiferman, 1970; Harper and Sanders, 1975; Lever, 1976; Polgar, 1976; Borman, 1979; and Parnell and Ketterson, 1980). Therefore, the installation characteristics and safety status of this category of equipment is, for the most part, the primary barometer for the status of our park system's playgrounds.

Results for Swinging Equipment

A total of 398 swing structures representing 1,262 actual swing seats were evaluated. Swings comprised 22.8 percent of total equipment surveyed, with the typical park playground having an average of two swinging structures present representing approximately seven actual seats. Types of swings ranged from traditional suspension swings to exer-gliders and platform swings and to swings with action in more than one direction (e.g. tire swings).

Implications for Safety

The USCPSC (1980a) has noted that swings account for the second highest number of injuries on playgrounds (23 percent of total injuries). Of the 1,262 seats available in this sample, 328 or 26 percent (26%) of these were metal or wooden seats. This finding is disturbing given the USCPSC data which indicates that 26 percent of all swing injuries resulted when children were struck by a moving swing. The presence of hard wooden/metal seats will continue to cause these kinds of injuries.

The average distance between swing seats was 26 inches, which is well in excess of the 18-inch minimum clearance recommended by USCPSC. However, in light of the fact that 16 percent (representing 131 total seats) of all swing seats were swivel seats, (which allow for rota-lateral movement by the child while swinging) the wider margin of clearance would be needed in order to avoid collisions by two children swinging side by side.

Fifty-nine percent (59%) of park playgrounds provided swing seats designed specifically for younger children (e.g. lower swing seats, seats with sides, backs, and/or safety bars or belts). Not all of these however were provided on a separate structure; only 45 percent of park playgrounds provided for such design considerations for their younger users (children under five). Thus, in some instances younger children could only access seats designed for them by traversing through the same traffic patterns as older users, or in many instances had to settle for seats designed for older users.

Perhaps most disappointing is the finding that 89 percent of park playgrounds did not provide for a barrier in the design and layout of their swinging equipment. Without a barricade to route traffic around swings in motion the likelihood of injury from swing impact remains high. Lack of barriers is particularly serious in light of the findings above which indicate that younger children must frequently mix-in with older children to use swings, and that one in four swing seats are metal or wood.

Over 98 percent of all swinging structures were firmly anchored; however, swings on one in four playgrounds were found to have sharp edges or projections in excess of USCPSC guidelines and over one in four playgrounds had swing structures (27%) which had moving parts that were not in good repair. Of those seats suspended by chains only 20 percent had safety coverings to protect pinch points.

Finally, Figure 5.1 illustrates that over 25 percent of the surfaces under swinging structures do not meet impact attenuation recommendations. Research has demonstrated surfaces such as concrete, asphalt, and packed clay to be the poorest and most dangerous (Beine and Sorrels, 1979; Rutherford, 1979). Additionally, grass undersurfaces which are subject to both weather and user erosions rapidly can become packed clay unless rigorously maintained. Since over 69 percent of all injuries related to swings occur from falls to the surface, (USCPSC 1980a, p. 3) and since impact attenuation data on surfacing has been available since the late 1970s, the fact that such a high percentage of swinging structures are still installed over hard surfaces is, from a safety viewpoint, absolutely negligent.

Swing Safety Summary

A significant proportion of swinging structures in park playgrounds pose serious safety concerns. The continued use of hard wooden/metal seats (26 percent of all seats), lack of swings for younger children (41%), mixing of age groups on swinging structures (55%), lack of safety barriers around swing arcs (80%), number of structures with protruding bolts or sharp edges (25%), number of seats with unsafe moving parts (27%), and lack of safety sheathing on swings suspended by chains, along with the installation of swings over hard unsafe fall surfaces paints a very disappointing picture of these popular play structures. These concerns are summarized graphically in Figure 5.2.

On a more positive note, the fact that 98 percent of all swing structures were firmly anchored and that the actual distance between seats exceeded USCPSC safety guidelines is slightly encouraging.

Surface Type	Sand	Mulch	Pea Gravel	Rubber Matting	Grass	Clay	Asphalt	Concrete	Other
% of Playgrounds	40%	9%	10%	.5%	12%	9%	3%	1%	15.5%

Represent acceptable surfaces for impact attenuation if installed and maintained at acceptable depth of surface to height of swinging arc ratio.

Represent surfaces ranging from totally unacceptable and unsafe (e.g. clay, asphalt, concrete) to surfaces with high potential to become unsafe, due to wear and weather erosion.

Figure 5.1 Surfacing Materials Found Under Swings

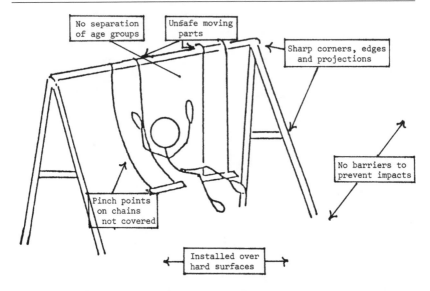

Figure 5.2 Problems with Swinging Structures

Results for Slides

A total of 378 pieces of sliding equipment, representing over 21.6 percent of total equipment in use, were evaluated. Types of slides included traditional flat slides, tube slides, and spiral slides, with each playground providing an average of 1.9 slide installations, the vast majority of which (81%) were traditional flat slides. The USCPSC (1980a) data indicated injuries from slides accounted for 16 percent of all playground injuries making them third highest in total number of injuries generated. Seventy-eight percent (78%) of these injuries were the result of falls over the side.

Implications for Safety

For the most part park slides were found to be well installed (92% percent firmly anchored) and well maintained with little broken equipment (only 8%) and few sharp edges or protrusions (16%). Additionally, over 93 percent were found to have a safe sliding surface and most (80%) had an angled deceleration chute at the end of the slide to facilitate a safe and controlled landing.

However, only 28 percent of all slides had a wide enough sliding surface to accommodate more than one child at a time and over half

(53%) did not provide the recommended 13 inches at the top of the chute for safe slide exit behaviors (USCPSC 1980a). Thus by design, over two thirds, 72 percent of all slides, have the potential (in the absence of turn taking behaviors) to facilitate crowding on the ladder or platform since only one child can slide at a time. This potential for crowding is further exacerbated by the lack of a guard rail on the platform in 11 percent of all slides evaluated. Additionally, insufficient height at the chute exit point might delay children from exiting, thus creating the potential for collisions (for example, without enough room to bend the knees and stand, children either delay exiting or fall back onto the slide chute as a result of a failed exit attempt; in either instance, it leaves open the possibility for colliding with the movement of the next user(s) down the chute).

The vast majority of slides were low to the ground (68 percent eight feet and under) or of moderate height (18 percent eight to ten feet high). However, some 6 percent of slides were 10 to 11 feet high, and 8 percent were in excess of 11 feet. This information regarding excessive height when coupled with the under surface data presented in Figure 5.3, represents a troubling scenario. Twenty (20%) percent of the surfaces that slides were installed over do not provide the cushion potential necessary to attenuate impact force that would be generated by a fall from a high platform.

In light of injury data in which users losing balance, losing grip and/or roughhousing behavior clearly contributed to falls (USCPSC, 1980a, p. 3), slide heights of ten feet and greater and hard impact surfaces underneath slide structures seem unnecessarily precarious and negligent.

Slide Safety Summary

The vast majority of slides are properly installed and safely maintained. Still, the installation of slides designed to accommodate more

Surface Type	Sand	Mulch	Pea Gravel	Rubber Matting	Grass	Clay	Asphalt	Concrete	Other
% of Playgrounds	44%	9%	11%	1.5%	11%	8%	.5%	1%	14.5%

Represent acceptable surfaces for impact attenuation if installed and maintained at acceptable depth of surface to height of platform ratio.

Represent surfaces ranging from totally unacceptable and unsafe (e.g. clay, asphalt, concrete) to surfaces with high potential to become unsafe, due to user and weather erosion.

Figure 5.3 Surfacing Materials Found Under Slides

than one child at a time would eliminate one potential source for safety concern, namely crowding behavior. Since only one-fourth (28%) of total structures accommodate such use at present, there is room for considerable improvement in this area. An additional design problem with slides in current use is insufficient ground clearance at the chute exit point. Over half of the current installations (53%) fail to provide for efficient and safe exits.

Certainly, the most problematic areas needing attention are the number of high slides still in operation (14 percent ten feet or higher), along with unacceptably hard surfaces found underneath 20 percent of existing installations. Particularly where these two conditions exist together, they could, with the use of concrete, for example, cause very serious or even fatal, injuries for users. Figure 5.4 summarizes safety concerns for slides found on park playgrounds.

Climbing Equipment

A total of 426 pieces of climbing equipment, representing nearly one-quarter (24.4%) of total equipment in use, were evaluated. This was a very heterogeneous category and types of equipment included:

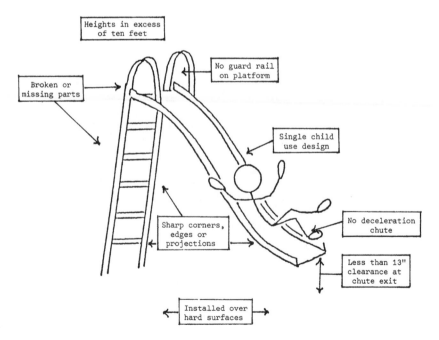

Figure 5.4. Problems with Slides

41 geodesic dome climbers (9.6%), 95 fireman poles (22.3%), 66 monkey bars (15.4%), 41 parallel bars (9.6%), 92 overhead ladders (21.6%), and 91 chinning bars (21.4%). On the typical park playground, one would expect to find at least two different pieces of climbing equipment. The USCPSC data (1980a) indicate that injuries from climbing equipment account for 42 percent of all injuries suffered on play equipment. Analysis of these injuries reveals that falls are responsible for nearly three-fourths (72%) of accident reports. Swinging, stunting, and jumping behaviors while on climbing supports were the most noted contributors for loss of grip or balance leading to injury.

Implications for Safety

The vast majority of climbing apparatus were firmly anchored in place (99%) and had component parts securely fastened together (92%). However, there were several design, installation, and maintenance issues evident. Nearly one-fifth (19%) of climbing apparatus had finger trap openings, and injuries from such openings have ranged from cuts and lacerations up to traumatic amputation of the digit in some cases (Rutherford, 1979). Additionally, 13 percent of these structures had dangerous sharp edges or protrusions and some 14 percent had V angles less than the USCPSC recommendations (at least 7 inches between angled parts) leaving open the possibility of head, body part, or clothing entrapment by users (several deaths by asphyxiation and strangulation have occurred nationally due to these design deficiencies).

Contributing to design problems inherent in many of the climbing apparatus evaluated are the data dealing with function and use. The average hand hold diameter of 2.53 inches exceeds the USCPSC (1980b) standard of 1.6 inches by almost a full inch. Similarly the 19.6 inches average distance between levels is well in excess of the USCPSC recommendation of no more than 7 to 11 inches distance (USCPSC, 1980b, p. 15). These two findings together thus render use of most climbing equipment by children five or younger (the anthropomorphic basis for USCPSC standards) at best difficult, if not dangerous. The great distances between levels and large hand hold grips together would greatly increase the tendency for younger children to lose their grip or balance while using the equipment.

Regarding equipment height, most structures were at a safe height (average of 7.4 feet) with the majority (82%) under nine feet and another ten percent not over ten feet. However, additional structures at 12 feet, (3%) 13 feet (1%) and 15 feet or greater (4%) represent a total of 30 structures in the survey sample that provide for excessive height. As was the case with sliding structures, the potential for excessively high structures occurring in concert with dangerously hard undersurfaces exists for climbers, as well. Figure 5.5 summarizes surface materials. Once again, completely unacceptable surfaces (6% on concrete, asphalt or clay) and surfaces of questionable impact attenuation value (21% grass) leave open the possibility of increased injuries from falls. Given the knowledge found in the national injury data base (recall 42 percent of total injuries on climbers with 72 percent of these suffered in falls to the undersurface), these data are particularly disappointing.

Climbing Equipment Safety Summary

The majority of climbing apparatus evaluated were firmly anchored, free of broken or loose parts, and installed at a safe height over acceptable surface materials. However, a significant minority of such equipment still provide opportunity for serious injury through finger trap openings, tight V intersections, excessive heights, and dangerous, hard undersurfaces. In addition, given the heterogenous nature of park clientele, young children attempting to use the typical climbing apparatus would appear to be at greater risk of injury due to the average large hand hold and excessive distance between level dimensions found. By design, these features will lead to a greater incidence of failed movement attempts and possible injury by younger children. The question of design fit for younger children represents a less apparent safety issue than a broken or loose component part, but nonetheless, is a real issue. Parents/caregivers might readily spot a poor installation or broken part, but may not be perceptive to the possibility of needing to rescue a young child who is frozen at and/or about to fall from a precarious height (the so called "kitten up a tree" crises which occur all too often when young children use equipment designed for older users) (Gabbard and LeBlanc, 1980). Figure 5.6 summarizes the current safety concerns with climbing apparatus evident from this survey of park playgrounds.

Surface Type	Sand	Mulch	Pea Gravel	Rubber Matting	Grass	Clay	Asphalt	Concrete	Other
% of Playgrounds	43%	9%	7%	1%	21%	2%	2%	2%	13%

Represent acceptable surfaces for impact attenuation if installed and maintained at acceptable depth of surface to climber height.

Represent surfaces ranging from totally unacceptable and unsafe (e.g. clay, asphalt, concrete) to surfaces with high potential to become unsafe, due to wear and weather erosion.

Figure 5.5 Surfacing Materials Found Under Climbing Apparatus

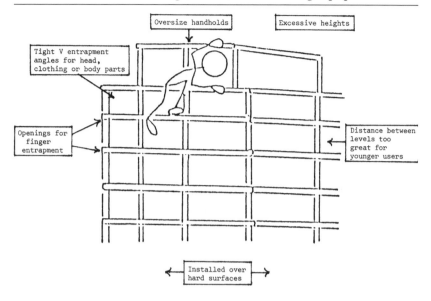

Figure 5.6 Problems With Climbers

Implications Based On Theories Of Play

Regardless of theoretical orientation, most people would agree that children are strongly shaped and directed by their environment. What about the outdoor play environment as it relates to theory? Children have shown us, by their choices, that they prefer this category of equipment over others we offer on the playground as evidenced by traffic pattern and use studies. (Van Alstyne, 1932; Wade, 1968; Brown, 1978 and Gabbard and LeBlanc, 1980.) They are also showing us through their behaviors that use of such equipment is hazardous to them. USCPSC injury statistics clearly indicate this. Why? Is it the equipment design or the play style engaged in? Obviously the falls from stunting, jumping, and swinging behaviors which occur on these apparatus make some theories appear more relevant than others. For instance, consider arousal seeking, which asserts that children seek optimal sensation; or cathartic theory, which finds play the answer to the need to release aggression and/or built up dissonance; or even surplus energy theory, the key tenant of which holds that the expenditure of surplus energy is rewarding and enjoyable. It can be argued that any of these theories are supported, in part, by the injury and use data for climbers, swings, and slides. Certainly the vigorous gross motor activity required by these apparatus, in conjunction with the variety of forces (such as rapid acceleration and deceleration, wind rush, gravitational pulls from inverted body positions) and rich sensory experiences offered (such as, vestibular and proprioceptive channels) could be used as compelling arguments in support of these theories as possible motivators and hence contributors to injuries.

Yet, the nature of intrinsic forces which sustain behaviors is theoretically elusive and will be debated for some time to come. For the purpose of constructing safe and appropriate playgrounds, at a certain level, the question of *why* children play is not as important as *how* children play. The simple fact remains that the categories of equipment reviewed in this chapter remain the most readily available, most frequently used, and most collectively dangerous to our children.

What about the question, "How do the children play?" We know from simple descriptive research that children love to climb and given a choice of levels will increasingly strive to play at the highest available level (Karlson and Ellis, 1972). Therefore, when designing playgrounds for all ages, it only makes sense to set safe ceilings on heights to protect the youngest and most vulnerable climbers. Ellis (1973) has recorded that, given increased familiarity with a piece of equipment, children will inevitably seek novel ways to be involved with it. Thus, the contention that children use equipment inappropriately (USCPSC, 1980a) should in fact be viewed as an inappropriate "adult" concept of how children play and not at all representative of how we can expect children to behave. We know that children will naturally seek novelty in movement, and stunting behaviors are a natural progression of familiarity. We also know, from clearly descriptive research, that children display intentional behaviors. They organize their movement and work for a reward, whether it be a sensory reward desired from a particular inverted body position or a social reward from peers or adult onlookers. Ellis feels (1972, p. 50) that arousal seeking, which is a part of the range of intentional behaviors we can expect to see, is best facilitated in group settings. When you consider the data presented in this chapter, it clearly demonstrates that most slides will only accommodate a single child, and that group use of most swings is dangerous given the lack of safety barriers. A number of climbers are perilously high or installed over hard surfaces. The obvious conclusion is that equipment has been designed and installed which is in direct opposition to the play patterns which play theorists and researchers alike tell us can be expected from children.

Implications Based On Total Development

Certainly one of the most common arguments for the use of outdoor playgrounds is the claim that they facilitate gross motor development of children. Yet, the available traffic pattern studies for this category of equipment do not support high use patterns for middle and older childhood (Parnell and Ketterson, 1980; Gabbard and LeBlanc, 1980). Moreover, the data from this study clearly indicate that the majority of swings, climbers, and slides are anthropomorphically unsuitable for developmental play by younger children (for example, hand holds are too large and climbing levels too high). So, the logical question is, "Are children engaging in equipment play long enough to derive any motor development or physical fitness benefits?" It would appear not. In a recent national survey, the American Physical Therapy Association found that 50 percent of elementary aged school children failed the tests for balance and reaction time (Wallace, 1987). These findings, in conjunction with increasing obesity in children of all ages in the United States (Gortmaker, Dietz, Sobol, and Wehler, 1987), and decreasing activity levels (Timmer, Eccles, and O'Brien, 1983) leads to speculation as to whether or not children are physically fit and developmentally mature enough to become engaged with challenge apparatus like climbers, swings, and slides. With so many children physically unfit, yet developmentally driven toward novelty and risk taking (something considered a necessary and integral part of a child's total development) (Rutherford, 1979), it is little wonder that these types of equipment are responsible for so many injuries. Much of a child's decision-making process is based on previous experiences in falls versus near falls (Brown, 1978; Besson, 1979). With so many children failing national developmental norms for balance and reaction time, it is clear that many are impaired in negotiating risk taking decisions. Cumulatively, the research on risk taking behavior, when combined with injury analysis research and playground equipment characteristics as revealed in this study, clearly indicate a large disparity between children's perceptions of what they can do (confidence in moving) and their ability to perform (competence). We must respond to this professionally in at least two ways.

First, there is an urgent need to educate parents and/or caregivers who bring children to the playground. Adults need to be more involved, not just in the supervision of safe play, but also in leading children through the mental decision-making process of so called challenge play. Particularly with regard to young boys, research demonstrates that in body oriented environments like playgrounds (Erbaugh and Clifton, 1984) boys will tend to imitate models (copy stunts) more readily than will girls.

Secondly, extensive retrofits of existing playground structures with excessive heights and hard undersurfaces simply must take place. Today's generation of children are clearly at physical risk from these high structures and hazardous installations. Further, without more attention in the manufacture and installation of play equipment to correctly fit and accommodate the anthropomorphic features of what are, developmentally, the appropriate users (namely preschoolers), the usefulness of playgrounds as an adjunct to facilitating total development remains highly speculative.

Bibliography

Beine, W. B. and Sorrels, J. R. (1979, November). *Soil impact attenuation performance; a field study.* Center for Consumer Product Technology.

Besson, E. A. (1979, May). *Briefing memorandum; public playground equipment.* U.S. Consumer Product Safety Commission.

Borman, K. M. (1979, October). Children's interactions on playgrounds. *Theory Into Practice, 19 (4)* 251-7.

Brown, V. R. (1978, October). *Human Factors analysis of injuries associated with public playground equipment.* U.S. Consumer Product Safety Commission.

Ellis, M. J. (1973). *Why people play.* Englewood Cliffs, NJ: Prentice Hall Publishing Co.

Eiferman, R. R. (1970). Levels of children's play as expressed in group size. *British Journal of Educational Psychology, 40,* 161-70.

Erbaugh, S. J. and Clifton, M. A. (1984). Sibling relationships of preschool aged children in gross motor environments. *Research Quarterly for Exercise and Sport, 55(4),* 323-331.

Gabbard, C. P., and LeBlanc, E. (1980, May). Movement activity levels on traditional and contemporary playground structures. *ERIC/EDRS,* #198-082.

Gortmaker, S. L., Dietz, W. H., Sobol, A. M., and Wehler, C. A. (1987). Increasing Obesity in the United States. *American Journal of Diseases of Children, 141,* 535-40.

Harper, L. V. and Sanders, K. M. (1975). Preschool children's use of space; sex differences in outdoor play. *Developmental Psychology, 11(1),* 119-23.

Karlson, K. A., and Ellis, M. J. (1972). Height preferences of young children at play. *Journal of Leisure Research, 4,* 33-42.

Lever, J. (1976). Sex differences in games children play. *Social Problems, 23(4),* 479-88.

Parnell, I. and Ketterson, P. (1980, May). What should a playground offer? *The Elementary School Journal, 80(5),* 233-39.

Polgar, S. K. (1976, October). The social context of games: or when is play not play? *Sociology of Education, 49,* 265-71.

Rutherford, G. W. (1979, May). *HIA hazard analysis: injuries associated with public playground equipment.* U.S. Consumer Product Safety Commission.

Thompson, D. (1988). Slides, swings, and climbing equipment. In L. D. Bruya & S. J. Langendorfer (Eds.), *Where our children play, (1).* Reston, VA: AAHPERD.

Timmer, S. G., Eccles, J., and O'Brien, K. (1983). How children use time. In F. T. Juster and RIP. Stafford (eds.), *Time, goods, and well-being.* Ann Arbor: Institute for Social Research.

U.S. Consumer Product Safety Commission, (1980a). *A handbook for public playground safety, (Vol. 1: General guidelines for new and existing playgrounds).* Washington, D.C.: U.S. Government Printing Office.

U.S. Consumer Product Safety Commission, (1980b). *A handbook for public playground safety, (Vol. II: Technical Guidelines for equipment and surfacing).* Washington, D.C.: U.S. Government Printing Office.

Van Alstyne, D. (1932). *Play behavior and choice of materials of preschool children.* Chicago: University of Chicago Press.

Wade, G. R. (1968). A study of free-play patterns of elementary school age children on playground equipment. (Unpublished masters thesis.) Pennsylvania State University, *ERIC/EDRS,* #187-791.

Wallace, L. (1987). Childrens poor physical condition is leading cause of sports injuries. *JOPERD, 58(3),* 19.

6

Rotating, Spring Rocking and Seesaw Equipment

by Marcia Carter

This chapter focuses on data in sections 7, 8, and 9 of the survey instrument. Specifically, data are concerned with rotating (section 7), spring rocking (section 8), and seesaw (section 9) equipment. Rotating equipment includes merry-go-rounds and swinging gates which rotate around a center fulcrum. Spring rocking equipment includes horses and similar toys which are fixed to stationary posts that allow either forward-backward, up-down, or side-to-side motions due to a spring mechanism. Seesaw equipment includes the seesaw, better known as a teeter totter, which is a beam (lever) tilting around a center point (fulcrum).

Also discussed in the chapter will be safety implications for all children who use park playgrounds. Data from the U.S. Consumer Product Safety Commission (USCPSC) playground studies (1979, p.3) are cited as reference criteria. Further, data from the survey will be discussed in view of the play theories. Why children play with these three types of equipment will be explored with reference to particular interpretations of the meaning of play. Implications for the development of all children will be proposed.

Rotating Equipment Data Summary

There were 97 total pieces of rotating equipment like merry-go-rounds on the 198 community parks surveyed in the 18 states. This represents less than one piece of rotating equipment on every two (49%) community parks surveyed or approximately 5.5 percent of the total pieces of observed equipment. Thus, merry-go-rounds and swinging gates comprise a small proportion of all equipment available to youth in community parks.

A majority (or 96 percent of the 97 pieces of rotating equipment) were firmly anchored in the ground with most (94%) securely fastened at their joints. Thus, while in operation, most of the equipment was safe from coming loose.

Over one-fourth (28%) of the rotating equipment had either sharp edges or projections which could puncture or cut. Additionally nearly half (46%) had open areas around the rotation post where limbs could be trapped during equipment operation. Only a third (32%) had a safety clearing of 20 feet for entering and exiting this equipment area in the parks.

Surfaces found under the 97 pieces of rotating equipment were predominately categorized as loose materials, sand (42%) and pea gravel (14%). Together with grass (10%) these surfaces comprised two-thirds (66%) of the materials found under rotating equipment. Hard surfacing materials such as concrete (1%), asphalt (5%) and materials that compact with either use or weather, clay (9%) and mulch (9%) were observed on less on than one-fourth (24%) of the community parks (see Figure 6.1).

Rotating Equipment Safety Implications

The USCPSC playground studies (1979, p. 3), cited merry-go-rounds as 5 percent of the playground equipment in use with 8 percent of the injuries attributed to this particular type of equipment. Most of the injuries resulted from falls when participants either lost their grips and were thrown from the merry-go-round, fell down while pushing it, or fell while riding it (1979, p.4). Some were struck while pushing the merry-

Surface Materials Under Rotating Equipment

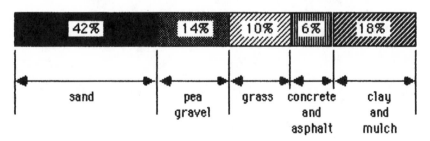

Figure 6.1 Loose materials comprised 66 percent of the surfaces under rotating equipment.

go-round. Those who fell while on the apparatus either struck or were struck by gripping bars or struck the base itself (1979, p.4).

Data from the surveyed community parks identify three general safety concerns. Minor to major injuries could result from sharp corners, edges, or projections; entrapment or clothing entanglement around the rotation post; and from falls, blows, or being struck by either moving equipment or from the limited perimeter running space.

Spring Rocking Equipment Data Summary

In the 198 community parks, 192 rocking pieces of equipment were observed. This represents a piece of rocking equipment in nearly all parks (97%) and the third most frequent piece of equipment observed among the total (11%) equipment. Only swing structures and flat slides were more predominant than spring rockers in the surveyed parks. Thus, the safety and use of this equipment during play is potentially significant.

Safety evaluation of rocking equipment was overall positive. Data reported that 91 percent of the supports were firmly anchored to the ground; 78 percent of the equipment had all parts present and 83 percent had all parts securely fastened together. The results of the survey also noted that 76 percent of the spring rockers had two 3-inch long hand holds while 78 percent had proper size foot rests (4x6 inches). Yet, more than one-third of the equipment had either edges, protrusions (41%), or spring action (37%) that could injure riders.

Surface materials under 33 pieces of rocking equipment were studied. Results of the observations were similar to the findings of rotating equipment. Loose materials, sand (46%) and pea gravel (13%) were most evident. Together with grass (10%) these materials represented over two-thirds (69%) of the materials found under rocking equipment. Hard surface materials such as concrete (5%) and materials that compact with use or weather, clay (9%) and mulch (3%), were identified in less than one-fifth (17%) of the community parks (see Figure 6.2).

Spring Rocking Equipment Safety Implications

Safety features of spring rocking equipment were generally good. Yet, the possibility exists that users could be lacerated or punctured from sharp pieces and that fingers or feet could be caught in the spring device. In 17% of the surveyed community parks, there is potential for participant injury with falls to either hard surfaces or surfaces which lose their cushioning effect with weather and use.

SCCCC - LIBRARY
4601 Mid Rivers Mall Drive
St. Peters, MO 63376

Surface Materials Under Spring Rocking Equipment

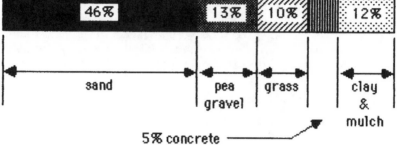

Figure 6.2 Loose materials comprised 69 percent of the surface found under spring rocking equipment.

Seesaw Equipment Data Summary

There were only 70 seesaws found in the 198 community parks. This figure suggests that a seesaw is found on approximately one in every three (35%) community parks. Seesaws represent only 4 percent of the total play structures found in the sampled community parks.

A majority of the seesaws (98%) were firmly anchored to the ground, over three-fourths (79%) had the required two 3-inch hand holds at each end, and nearly three-fourths (71%) had parts that were securely fastened together. Several features of either the seesaws or use of the seesaws could result in safety concerns. Over half (60%) of all seesaws assessed were built so that fingers or toes could be trapped or pinched by pivotal moving parts during operation. Further, over half (57%) of the seesaws permitted the body to pass underneath the equipment during its action. More than one-third (35%) also had sharp edges or projections. On only 17 percent of the assessed equipment was there provision for cushioning of the seesaws upon impact with the ground. The average height which a seesaw seat could reach was 3.8 feet from ground level.

Surface materials found under 70 pieces of seesaw equipment were similar to that found under both rotating and spring rocking equipment. Loose materials, sand (33%) and pea gravel (16%) with grass (20%) represented over two-thirds (69%) of the materials found under seesaws. Hard surface materials such as asphalt (4%) and materials that compact with use or weather, clay (2%) and mulch (9%) were identified as being used in less than one-fifth (15%) of the surveyed community parks (see Figure 6.3).

Seesaw Equipment Safety Implications

The USCPSC playground studies (1979, p.3), reported seesaws as 6 percent of the playground equipment in use with 5 percent of the injuries attributed to this particular piece of equipment. Most of these injuries resulted from falls; children were hit by moving seesaws; and others were injured by poorly maintained seesaws (1979, p.4).

Seesaws found in the community parks presented the possibility of major safety hazards. Participants may receive minor injuries from sharp edges, corners, and protruding wood or metal pieces. Additionally, their fingers or toes may become pinched or trapped by moving parts of the seesaw. Major injuries may result when participants fall beneath the seesaw on surfaces that become more compact or firm with use and under certain weather conditions.

Play Theories Related to Rotating, Spring Rocking and Seesaw Equipment

During three time periods since the late 20th century, attempts to explain the motive of play have been proposed by theorists and researchers. Classical theories of play evolved in the late 1800s and early 1900s and each attempted to provide explanations for behavior that was not considered work. These included the surplus energy, instinct, recapitulation, preparation, and relaxation theories. Theories proposed during the first half of this century (recent theories) were concerned with play content and cause and effect relationships. These

Surface Materials Under See Saws

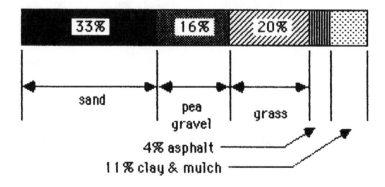

Figure 6.3 Loose materials comprised 69 percent of the surface found under see saws.

recent theories included generalization, compensation, catharsis, psychoanalytic, development, and learning. Two more recent theories of competence motivation and arousal seeking evolved from research of the 1960s. These attempt to explain why play occurs after needs are satisfied.

Six of these theories appear to have implications for play in community park playgrounds. Specifically, play on merry-go-rounds, spring rockers, and seesaws may be related to catharsis, psychoanalysis, developmental, learning, competence motivation, and arousal seeking behaviors. Catharsis theory proposes that frustration is expressed through play to reduce stress. The make believe play of riding a horse (spring rocker) or conquering another by having the advantage of being above or higher than another on the seesaw could relieve tension in a socially acceptable manner. The psychoanalytic theory contends that play is motivated by unpleasant experiences. Play on the merry-go-round and spring rocker offers role reversal opportunities. For example, the player in the new role of captain controls the flying saucer or horse. In this manner the unpleasantness of compliance with adult rules may serve as the motivator for this particular play experience.

Play is a child's first teacher. As the intellect develops, developmental theory relates that the play of children becomes more complicated. Through experience the child assimilates information such as the concepts of turning around, up-down or bounce. When a children's play begins to accommodate that of others, the child learns that as a result of cooperation, the merry-go-round moves faster or that everyone is included. Psychosocial development results from the child interacting with the environment and with others through the experiences of play.

Learning theorists suggest that play is response to reinforcers such as adults clapping when the child bounces (spring rocker), or pushing the merry-go-round faster. Moving equipment such as the merry-go-round, spring rocker, and seesaw stimulate behaviors due to their features. Children can explore, investigate, manipulate, and problem-solve following their use. These qualities are believed to be explained by the competence motivation and arousal seeking theories. Competence motivation is examplified in one child's attempt to control another by pushing the seesaw seat down. Pushing the merry-go-round faster or bouncing higher on the spring rocker may explain the child's attempt to experience the novelty of motion stimuli (arousal seeking theory).

Developmental Implications of Rotating, Spring Rocking and Seesaw Equipment

Development in social, cognitive, affective, and psycho-motor behaviors occurs through play. The spring rocker permits either extra-individual or aggregate social behavior. When one child is bouncing on one spring rocker, the action is extra-individual (action directed by one person toward an object in the environment). If several children are each bouncing on their own rockers without verbalizing or physically interacting with others on the spring rockers, their action is aggregate or parallel play. Action on the merry-go-round also may be either extra-individual or aggregate. The action of two children on a seesaw is representative of intra-group social behavior (action of a cooperative nature by two or more persons intent upon reaching a common goal). The simplest form of social interaction is extra-individual with aggregate and intra-group each requiring higher levels of social interaction. Thus, play may enhance social development.

The process of activity analysis is used to identify the behavioral requirements of activities. Within each behavioral domain, cognitive, affective, and psycho-motor, skills and abilities necessary to successfully complete an activity are listed by degree of difficulty or complexity. Most activities require skills in all three domains; yet in some, one domain is more dominant than the others. This results from the activity either requiring a larger number of skills or a higher level of skills in one particular domain. Moving play equipment requires the use of higher level skills in all three domains. In the cognitive area, the participant must use judgment and decision-making which is apparent when the participant moves either faster around or higher up and down or adjusts the seesaw leverage by moving forward or backward on the seat. The participant has made a decision that this action is safe given present skill levels. In the affective domain, the participant exhibits ego strength or confidence when not fearing either the speed of the merry-go-round, or height of the spring rocker or seesaw. Sensory-motor skills required on moving equipment include not only the fundamental skills of balancing, turning, grasping-releasing, sitting, climbing, and walking, but also such complex skills as dynamic balance, stamina, vestibular and proprioceptive perception, sensory discrimination, and postural and visual integration. Thus, use of moving equipment may enhance cognitive, affective, and sensory-motor skill development.

Therapeutic Implications of Play on Rotating, Spring Rocking, and Seesaw Equipment.

Play on moving equipment permits imitation, exploration, testing, and nonverbal expression. Also, this play is natural or normal. Using such equipment in parks also allows individual, parallel, and cooperative or group play. Children with special needs and varying ability levels may benefit from experiences involving this equipment. When modeling others, children learn by doing. Such skills as bouncing, sitting, and pushing are repeated over and over until they become a part of the skill repertoire of children.

Simultaneously, the children become familiar with the ways various body parts work and what they can and cannot do. Play on this equipment is also a form of self-validation or self-testing. Children, through active participation, learn the effects of actions like pushing or bouncing. Play does not require verbal interaction to assure success. Thus, nonverbal and gestural movements become a communication form. Play is a natural teacher. Participants learn to attend, to discriminate and to comprehend the meanings of such concepts as slow or fast, high and low, or up and down. All children play, regardless of ability level. Children with disabilities may experience limitations in their social and living environments, yet are capable of using moving equipment in community parks if it is accessible to them. Lastly, play on these pieces may be done alone, among and/or with others. This accommodates the three levels of social skill development.

Summary and General Implications

Spring rockers are more prevalent on community park playgrounds than either merry-go-rounds or seesaws. Three features in either construction or use present safety concerns with this moving equipment. Equipment design permitted users' limbs to be trapped or their clothes to be tangled while using the equipment. Equipment design and maintenance also allowed either pinching, puncturing, and/or cutting of users' limbs from sharp corners, edges, or projections. Surfaces found under each of the three types of equipment were predominately categorized as loose materials (sand, pea gravel or grass). These surface have advantages over hard surface materials such as concrete or asphalt in providing a cushion for falls; yet they too can have disadvantages which become especially noticeable after rain, humid conditions, and wind. These conditions may contribute to a reduction in cushioning or padding capability of the materials. A fall to a weathered or well packed surface can also be dangerous.

Play theories present alternatives to the question "why play?" Six theories, catharsis, psychoanalytic, developmental, learning, competence motivation, and arousal seeking, appear to provide some justification for play. However, none adequately interprets all play behavior. Combined, these theories provide some explanation for why playgrounds are void of playing children. The qualities in moving equipment that create opportunities for imitation, exploration, and novelty are limited and thus present concern for the utility of traditional community park playground equipment.

Value of park playgrounds would appear to be in their potential to support growth and development of children of all ability levels. Play is a tool through which important life skills are acquired and practiced. Cognitive, affective, and psychomotor skills are enhanced through play. Use of merry-go-rounds, spring rockers, and seesaws requires complex high level abilities in each of these domains. Thus, the range of use of this equipment as therapeutic tools could be quite broad.

Bibliography

Avedon, E. M. (1974). *Therapeutic recreation service, an applied behavioral science approach.* Englewood Cliffs, NJ: Prentice-Hall, Inc.

Bruya, L. D. & Langendorfer, S. J. (eds) (1988). *Where our children play, elementary school playground equipment.* Reston, VA: American Alliance for Health, Physical Education, Recreation and Dance.

Ellis, M. J. (1973). *Why people play.* Englewood Cliffs, NJ: Prentice-Hall, Inc.

Fein, G. (1979). Play in acquisition of symbols. In L. Katz (Ed.), *Current topics in early childhood education.* Norwood, NJ: Ablex.

Frost, J. L. (1985). *Toward an integrated theory of play: The young child and music.* Wheaton, MD: Association for Childhood Education International.

Piaget, J. (1962). *Play, dreams and imitation in childhood.* New York: W. W. Norton.

Rubin, K. H., Maioni, T. L. & Hornung, M. (1976). Free play behaviors in middle- and lower-class preschoolers: Parten and Piaget revisited. *Child Development, 47,* 414-419.

7

Sand Play Containers, Wading Pools, Signs, Trees and Pathways

by Frances Wallach

While the U.S. Consumer Product Safety Commission Guidelines focus on playground equipment and the surface beneath it , children gravitate toward playing in and with natural materials in the environment. Sand, water, and vegetation fascinate youngsters, since they provide the setting for both creative play and social interaction. These represent play opportunities in which the participants direct and control their own destinies by manipulating the natural materials into their own imaginative play. Just as in the free-soaring creativity of the adventure playgrounds, referred to by Ellis (1973), children can dig, build, adapt to their environment, and learn the true meaning of cooperative play.

Sand Play

Sand, reports Mason (1982) is the easiest way to introduce the quality of change into the play environment. Sand can continually change form as it is dug, mounded, and moved. As a loose material, it introduces change but is socially acceptable and, according to Mason, aesthetically unimposing. Sand is a favorite play involvement for very young children, and sandboxes are typical in nursery school settings. It is also one of the play opportunities in which all children, including those with disabilities, can participate. Thus playgrounds seeking to serve all children will include sand play areas, both at ground level and in raised containers for those in wheelchairs. Sand play is the great equalizer, where age differences, size, muscle development, and strength make no impact on social interaction. All varieties of youngsters learn to cooperate in sand play. When sand play areas are not provided on the playground, children will dig into the loose surfaces under play equipment to replace the lost opportunity of designated sand play.

Sand play areas can be divided into two categories: the smaller "sand table" or "sandbox," in which the play is primarily manipulative and imaginative; and the larger sand "play area," large enough for children to walk around in, jump, run, and enjoy physical growth and freedom. Sand play areas, however, are not as common in park playgrounds as might be expected. Of the 198 community parks surveyed, only 30 had sand play areas and the actual sizes of these areas are undefined. Bruya and Langendorfer (1988), in reporting on the AAHPERD Committee on Play study of elementary school playgrounds, indicated that there were 41 sand play areas on 206 playgrounds—a finding which matches that in community parks.

Of all the equipment pieces in the play area, sand play areas in parks constituted only 1.7 percent of the play opportunities, a slightly better percentage than found in schools (1.3%)—information acquired from the AAHPERD study conducted one year earlier. (Bruya and Langendorfer, 1988.)

With sand play being recognized universally as an excellent play experience, it would seem that sand play areas would be far more popular in playground installations. However, the maintenance problems, and the attention needed to provide safe sand play areas discourage operating agencies from including them in the design of the playgrounds. Failure to maintain sand play areas can lead to health hazards, rather than accidents, but these health hazards can be far more critical. Neglected sand play areas can transmit serious diseases to a large number of users, as compared to the accident involving a single child on play equipment. In addition, sand becomes a physical hazard, since it is easy to slip on when it spills on the concrete or asphalt (*Play for All Guidelines*, 1987).

Playgrounds	Playgrounds in Survey	No. of Sand Play Areas	% of Sand Play Areas
Schools	206	41	19.9
Parks	198	30	15.1

Figure 7.1 - Section 10: *Sand Play Areas*

Item	% Yes	% No
Clean and debris free	59	41
Good drainage apparent	55	45
Covered or located to exclude animals	19	81
Adult seating available	75	25

Figure 7.2 - Section 10: *Percentages for 30 Designated Sand Play Areas*

The basic problems with the use of sand are primarily those of maintenance. Animal feces, glass, sharp objects and other debris are both disease and injury-causing if not removed. Placing covers on sand areas can cause dampness, mold, and a haven for insects. Of the 30 sand play areas reviewed in community parks, the findings in Figure 7.2 illustrate the level of concern by the operating agencies.

In addition to the proper maintenance that is required—daily raking and cleaning—there are other safety precautions which can help to keep the sand play area safe. Seating for adult supervision, to watch over children as they play, was present in only 75 percent of the sand play areas; and placing the sand play area away from the street or residential yards might make it less attractive to domestic animals (*Play for All Guidelines,* 1987). Proper containment of the sand, with high enough barriers to keep the sand from pouring over onto the outside surface, will ameliorate the slipping problem. Most desirable are the retaining barriers that have adult seating laid on top of them, with designated entrance points for children (Figure 7.3).

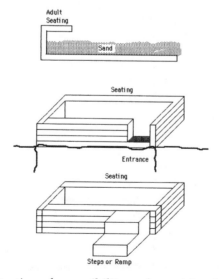

Figure 7.3 Illustration of accessibility and provision for adult seating

Raised sandboxes provide access for children in wheelchairs.

Nevertheless, sand play areas are critical components for creative play. The office of the Canadian Minister of National Health and Welfare (1984) lists the following activities that children love in sand play, and that are important to growth: heaping, pushing, pulling, smoothing, crawling, lying, kneeling, lifting, sitting, and digging. And, as children grow older, they add: building, planning, sculpting, and carving. While ground sand play areas are not accessible to wheelchairs, raised sandboxes can serve the same purposes for children with disabilities.

And, while the survey did not locate the sand play areas, it should be noted that sand and water play go hand-in-hand, and sand play areas should be located near a water source or water hydrant (Frost and Klein, 1979).

Swedlow (1968) points out that the attitudes, values, and skills that children gain through play help them develop not only a depth of understanding that gives meaning to formal learning, but also a concept of themselves as learning persons. If children are to develop competencies in reading, writing, and mathematics, it is necessary to develop: visual memory, auditory memory, language acquisition, classification, hand-eye coordination, body image, and spatial orientation. The skills and concepts needed to develop these abilities can be acquired with such open-ended materials as sand and water, and are learned while children play.

Both sand and water are prime materials for places that feel different, places for building, places for creative expression, and places for pretending (Greenman, 1988). The use of sand and water play provide key opportunities for exploration and manipulation. In reviewing the values identified with these experiences, the following is evident:

Exploration—allows the child to experience challenge, the sense of adventure, problem solving, identification of new objects and experiences.

Manipulation—provides experiences with configurations, shapes, patterns, spatial relationships, sequencing, and measurements.

Wading Pools

Water play, along with sand, constitutes a very small percentage of the play opportunities on the playground. Water is fascinating to children, in that it "plays back" and interacts with the children. Water is not static—it responds to movement. Its movements cannot be controlled by children and present a challenge to youngsters. Water, along with sand, constitutes play with "loose parts" (Nicholson, 1971). And, water presents an opportunity for physical growth, social development, and cognitive skill development. Children love to touch, feel, immerse, and move in water. Friedberg (1975) developed an activities matrix which is valid for both able-bodied and disabled youngsters, and which identified such development as learning through cooperation, participation, interpretation, role playing, and problem solving, through water play. Children in wading pools can promote physical development through jumping, wading, floating, and learning to swim. Children who soon become bored with playground equipment can spend hours in a wading pool.

Unfortunately, few facilities surveyed contained wading pools. In the 198 community parks there were only six wading pools identified, representing three percent of the equipment. Probably this figure is close to the school playground survey findings, although comparison is not possible, since the school survey did not identify the number of wading pools in school settings. It reviewed the condition of the pools, but included the wading pools in "water play areas."

There appear to be several reasons why wading pools are not as prevalent as their popularity would suppose. They require constant and vigilant maintenance; they must have supervision; and they are usable, in most of the country, only during limited times of the year due to weather conditions. Therefore, they represent an expensive capital investment, along with an expensive cost of maintenance.

Wading pools, if improperly maintained and supervised, can provide hazardous situations which can result in serious injury,

Item	% Yes	% NO
Fenced and gates	52	47
Clear and free of debris	79	21
Adult seating provided	71	29
Filled water - average depth - 15.5 inches		

Figure 7.4 - Survey Section 11: *Percentage for 6 Wading Pools*

disease transmission, or death. Both the physical surroundings and the design of the wading pools can be hazard causing. Adult seating (see Figure 7.4) in the area is critical for supervision, since children can slip in the wading pools, fall, and possibly drown, even in the average water depth of 15.5 inches which was reported in the community park survey of the six wading pools.

What hazards can be identified in wading pools?
1. Unfenced pools, allowing free access, at any time, to children in the area and to animals.
2. Poor drainage, which will lead to polluted water and the transmission of infectious diseases.
3. Untreated water, which will again pollute and transmit diseases.
4. Lack of daily maintenance and removal of debris from the wading pool and surrounding area.
5. Lack of adult seating; discouraging supervision at the wading pool.
6. Lack of signage which will:
    a. identify the ages and sizes of the children who may use the pool; and
    b. remind the adults that the wading pool *must* be supervised.

Poor design of the area can, therefore, be a safety concern, as is lack of maintenance for cleanliness. And the lack of an adult supervisor, sitting poolside, can mean the difference between life and death when a young child falls, hits his head, and goes under even the minimal amount of water in the wading pool. Keeping the water clean through regular testing, and sweeping the bottom for broken glass, tins, etc., can make the difference in safe operations of wading pools.

Signs

"Failure to Warn" appears in the majority of lawsuits that are filed pertaining to playground accidents, according to Bauer and Pineger (1987). And, even though children, by law, are not required to read, it appears from court decision, that the posting of signs warning of potential hazards or providing instructions for use, constitute "due care" on the part of the facility operator. From the *Play for All Guidelines* (1987) it is recorded that signs ensure good orientation, direct traffic flow, and alert users to the special features of equipment. Signs are currently being utilized, across the country, to provide instructions for proper use of equipment on the playground; and these signs are multi-purpose (see Figure 7.5), in that they provide the use directions, utilizing large symbols for children who do not read, and also serve as directions for adults who supervise the children, whether or not official, trained supervisors are present.

Instructional signage, however, is a fairly new concept on the playground and, in the schools, is part of a curriculum offering on safety, where elementary school-age children learn the rules of proper play and how to relate and adhere to the instructions and symbols on the signs.

Signs provide warnings of danger, instructions for usage, information about the rules of a playground, and identity of the facility. By reminding users of hazards, and by cautioning for proper use, the playground operator incorporates a risk reduction technique (Wallach, 1988). However, the survey results showed very little use of signage at play areas.

It should be noted that signs in playgrounds can accomplish the following:

• Instructions to children on proper usage,
• Instructions to parents on proper supervision,
• Reminders to supervisors on proper play,
• Warnings for unperceived hazards,
• Set the parameters for use of the area (age groupings, no pets, etc.),
• Establish the environment for safer play (no bare feet, don't use equipment when wet),
• Establish a feeling of security (directional signs),
• Establish a "due care" defense.

Also available, in educational settings, are curriculum signs which, through graphics and verbiage, are providing activity instruction on the play equipment. These are placed or hung on the equipment while

Item	% Yes	% No
Signs which give help	2	98
Signs which suggest restricted or limited use	11	89
Signs which prohibit animals	13	87

Figure 7.5 - Survey Section 11: *Signs*

the supervisor conducts formalized activities. They are utilized in school playgrounds, while community park settings are directed more towards free play and free choice in play.

The use of signage is growing and it is hoped that the survey results will stimulate increased use of signs in play areas.

Trees and Shade

Shade in the play area, whether by vegetation or structures, is essential for both children and adults. Children need a place as respite from the rays of the sun, and from the heat in warm weather; shaded areas provide a spot for rest and relaxation; and the lack of shaded areas may mean that the likelihood of parents remaining in the area to interact during play is lessened (Bruya and Langendorfer, 1988). Even the design of the play equipment itself can provide shade during play.

Trees are not only good for shade, they are play structures that have been universally regarded as the natural way to play. Tree climbing was a play activity long before commercially designed climbing pieces were placed in the playground. Trees houses are favorite places in which to hide or be alone (Singer and Singer, 1979). Trees are constantly changing entities, because of the seasonal vegetation changes, the constant growth, and the effects of weather and the environment. Trees, as play apparatus, are exciting, challenging, and always interesting.

The survey reports that over two-fifths (44%) of the 198 play-grounds had shade available from structures. And, the average number of trees on a community park playground was 14. However, there is no information on whether the trees were used for shade, for windbreak, or for play.

For safety on the playground, decisions must be made on the purpose of trees. If they are to be used for climbing they must be sturdy, with sturdy branches that will not break when children climb. There must be sufficient climbing opportunities so that a youngster can both climb up and come down. And, unless a play structure is specifically designed around a tree, don't have trees placed near structures, which would allow children to climb from one to the other (*Play for All Guidelines*, 1987).

Trees which are placed in the play area for shade purposes, not to be climbed, should be pruned to a height of 7 ft., so that branches that could encourage climbing are removed, and low hanging branches will not serve as protrusions that could severely damage an eye.

Pathways

The survey reports that a little over two-fifths (44%) of the parks had hard surfaces which could be used for wheel toys. It did not identify the width of the paths, and whether they would be accessible

Trees which are placed in the play area for shade purposes, not to be climbed, should be pruned to a height of 7 feet.

to wheelchairs. However, wheel play is an important component for play. Not only are these pathways an opportunity for tricycles, wagons, jump ropes, balls, and brooms, but they separate and define play areas; they direct traffic patterns; and they provide opportunity for gross motor development in riding, pedalling, walking, hopping, running, and skipping. Many games can be played on pathways and following pathways is a safe way to traverse the play area and keep out of the way of children in play equipment.

Implications

Sand and water play areas are exciting play and growth opportunities, but are not frequently included in community park playgrounds. While they foster the development of creativity, they also provide an opportunity for the development of fine motor skills (Bruya and Langendorfer, 1988). But, looking at the survey, we can assume that fine motor skill is not addressed in our community park playgrounds. Both affective and cognitive development also suffer when these facilities are not available. If these skills are to be properly addressed, future playground plans will have to include sand and water play areas. This will also mean the provision of additional supervision, especially for wading pools.

Because of the legal implications, the lack of signage in the playgrounds probably represents a vulnerability on the part of the playground operator. While the presence of instructional and warning signs do not enhance play, the signs set the parameters for proper use of the facility and are visible evidence of "due care" taken to protect the users. Bruya (1988) points out that lack of signage represents two missed opportunities—lack of support for administrators and play leaders, and lack of support of the play patterns of children.

Shade, being essential on the playground, both for children at play and for supervising adults, is not as available on the playgrounds as had been imagined. Better than half the facilities surveyed were without shade. Lack of shade reduces use of the equipment, constricts the time span of play, and allows children to tire easily. Most important, it reduces the presence of adult supervision on the playground. Future playgrounds should certainly contain shade areas, whether in structures or trees.

The lack of hard surfaces for wheel toys was evident in 56 percent of the playgrounds, reducing the physical development opportunities present in wheeled play, and restricting the accessibility of the play area to wheelchairs. Lack of such surfacing reduces the scope of the play experiences of children.

Conclusions

It is obvious that playground designers must pay more attention to the provision of play opportunities available in sand and water play. The constant flow and change of the environment is mirrored in these forms of play; other playground equipment cannot provide some of the unique experiences which sand and water play can stimulate. The use of trees on the playground, and the addition of pathways for wheeled toys, again expand the use of the playground and provide settings for the learning of skills in and around the playground equipment. Clearly, much can be done to enhance the play areas and to open new skill learning opportunities for youngsters.

Bibliography

Bauer, E. G. and Pineger, R. D. (1987). *The primer for playground safety*. Grinnell, IA: Ashley Scott & Assoc., 69

Bruya, L. D. (1988). Sand area, wading area, signs trees and pathways. In Bruya, L. D. and Langendorfer, S. J. (Eds.), *Where our children play*. Reston, VA: AAHPERD, 133-135, 156, 170-172, 174.

Canadian National Health and Welfare Office. (1984). Ottawa: CNHW.

Ellis, M. J. (1973). *Why people play.* Englewood Cliffs, NJ: Prentice Hall, Inc., 139.

Friedberg, M. P. (1975) *Handicapped playgrounds.* New York: Vintage Books

Frost, J. L. and Klein, B. L. (1979). *Children's play and playgrounds.* Boston, MA: Allyn and Bacon, 84

Moore, R. C., Goltsman, S. M., and Lacofano, D. S. (Eds.). (1987). *Play for all guidelines.* Berkley, CA: MIG Communications, 54-57, 126, 154-155.

Mason, J. (1982). *The environment of play.* West Point, NY: Leisure Press

Nicholson, S. (1971). How not to cheat children: The theory of loose parts. *Landscape Architecture.*

Singer, D. G. and Singer, J. L. (1977). *Partners in play: A step-by-step guide to imaginative play in children.* New York: Harper & Row.

Swedlow, R. (1986). Children Play, Children Learn. In McKee, J. S. (Ed.) *Play: Working partner of growth.* Wheaton, MD: A.C.E.I., 32-33.

Wallach, F. (1988, July). The Sign Told Me How to Play—Lesson in Risk Reduction. *School Business Affairs.*

8

Litigation and Playgrounds
by Annie Clement

Playground directors, managers, supervisors and other personnel, paid employees or volunteers, can be held legally liable for incidents occurring on a playground. Their liability can be traced to a number of legal theories, with negligence and intentional tort the theories most often appearing in the litigation. The chapter will review the legal theories of negligence and intentional torts; summarize a study of the patterns of playground litigation; reference the results of the survey of playground equipment accidents for parks contained in this document and the U.S. Consumer Product Safety Commission research and handbooks on public playground safety; and recommend a system of risk management for playground personnel.

Legal Theories

Negligence is "the omission to do something which a reasonable [person], guided by those ordinary considerations which ordinarily regulate human affairs, would do, or the doing of something which a reasonable and prudent [person] would not do." (Black's Law Dictionary). The elements of negligence are:

1. a legal duty of care;
2. breach of the legal duty;
3. the breach of the legal duty as the proximate cause of the injury, and;
4. substantial harm.

A legal duty of care means that playground personnel are responsible or obligated to behave in a certain manner. The legal duty exists in the supervisor-playground participant or the director-playground participant relationship. The legal duty is based upon the expected skill, knowledge, and capacity of the supervisor/director and is enforced equally for volunteers and employees.

The legal duty implies a minimal standard of care that all playground personnel must adhere to. A clear cut statement of what that standard of care should be is seldom stated in literature on physical activity. When that standard of care is published, as it is in certain medical procedures, the court will merely implement the standard. When it is not stated the court will use documents such as the U. S. Consumer Product Safety Commission handbooks, literature in general, previous cases, expert testimony, and considered good practice to fashion a standard of care for a particular situation.

When a legal duty exists and children are injured, the court must prove that the breach of the duty was the real cause of the injury. For negligence to be proved the injured party must have sustained substantial damage.

Intentional torts are also injuries caused by failure to act or by an act. By intentional is meant the person executing the act intended that the act should occur. There need not be an intent to harm; under intentional tort substantial damages need not exist. When a child, playing on the playground, intentionally bats the head or body of another child, an intentional tort has occurred; when a bat slips from the hands of the child hitting another child, negligence can occur. Negligence will occur only if the child hit by the bat sustains a substantial injury.

Patterns of Playground Litigation

The following was based upon an analysis of cases appearing on the Lexis Retrieval System as of February 1988, under the key words "tort" and/or "negligence," and "playgrounds." A case appeared on the system only after the case had gone to court, a decision had been rendered, and the decision was appealed. There is speculation as to the number of cases settled out of court or settled at some point in the court process; speculation is that from 70 to 100 incidents in which litigation was threatened exist for every case available on the retrieval system (see Figure 8.1). There are values of reporting only cases from the retrieval system: 1) It is an accurate paper record available for drawing valid research conclusions; 2) The most serious cases, and those in which professionals are most concerned, tend to appear here.

Research presented included 123 cases taken from 1960 to 1988. Twenty-six percent (26%) occurred between 1960-1969; 30 percent (30%) occurred between 1970-1979, and 44 percent (44%) occurred between 1980-1988. Although the percentages suggested that litigation was increasing at a rapid rate, it should be noted that 10 percent (10%) of the cases occurred in 1980; 7 $\frac{1}{2}$ percent (7.5%) in 1960, and 2 $\frac{1}{2}$ percent (2.5%) in 1986. Agencies in which the incidents occurred are:

Agency	Number of Cases	Percentage of Total
Elementary Schools	62	50%
City and Municipal	37	30%
Day Care	6	5%
Other including commercial, churches, resorts, and housing authorities	18	15%

Cases occurred in only 34 states, with nearly 50 percent of the litigation in Illinois (10.5%) Louisiana (16%), and New York (19%). Injured plaintiffs were males 65 percent of the time and females 32 percent of the time. Three percent (3%) of the cases could not be identified by sex. Injured boys were 2 to 16 years of age, with the largest single group 6 years of age; injured girls were 5 to 14 years of age, with the largest single group 7 years of age.

The activity in which the participant was engaged at the time of the injury which resulted in litigation is the single most significant element to professionals planning safe playground environments. The following categories have been created to classify injuries: equipment, sport, or participant behavior.

Forty (40%) of the above cases were won by plaintiffs (children); 60 (60%) were won by the school, teacher, or agency.

Note that over half of the cases involved equipment. Equipment failure tended to occur more often than did the misuse of equipment. Baseballs and bats accounted for seven percent (7%) of the injuries, no other sport or game was easily identified in the study. This may result from the fact that softball/baseball is played in a playground setting while few other sports use playgrounds. Children "acting out" or engaging in horseplay accounted for another large percentage of the injuries as noted in the participant behavior category.

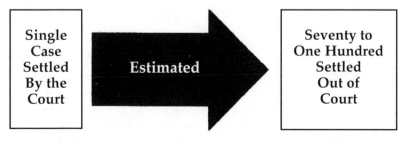

Figure 8.1 Many cases are estimated to exist in which litigation was threatened.

Table 8.1 Classification of injuries

Playground Equipment:	Number:	Percent:
Slide	18	15%
Monkey or Horizontal Bar	16	13%
Swing	13	10%
Merry-Go-Round	10	8%
See Saw	2	2%
Nonspecified	<u>4</u>	<u>3%</u>
	63	51
Sport:		
Hit by baseball	6	5%
Hit by bat	3	2%
Game called "Kill"	1	1%
Stick Ball	1	1%
Unspecified sport	<u>1</u>	<u>1%</u>
	12	10%
Participant Behavior:		
Throwing rocks	9	7%
Horseplay	6	5%
Walking on top of fence or guard rail	5	4%
Running into another child	5	4%
Fall from tree	5	4%
Fighting	4	3%
Fell in hole	3	2%
Crack the Whip	3	2%
Attempted to construct recently delivered playground equipment	1	1%
Hit by truck	1	1%
Hit by bicycle	1	1%
Hit by sled	1	1%
Eyes burned by lime	1	1%
Burned by high tension wire	1	1%
Sunburned	1	1%
Used father's ladder to remove ball from roof	<u>1</u>	<u>1%</u>
	48	39%

Research on Accidents

Various methods are used to track playground injuries. The most popular and the one used earlier in this document was the number of children treated in a hospital emergency room. The Consumer Product Safety Commission also used the hospital emergency treatment room as the indication of an accident. (It would seem that insurance coverage, socioeconomic level, and the availability of a parent would be factors in whether a child was taken to an emergency room.) The Consumer Product Safety Commission Directorate for Hazard Identification and Analysis (1979) stated that 72 percent of the injuries are the result of falls. They speculated that the falls resulted when children lost their grip or balance. They also noted that four out of five children were under ten years of age.

Given this information, professionals can easily ascertain that children are being asked to use equipment beyond their level of ability. Why has this occurred? Do parents and/or peers demand more than the child can handle or does the playground equipment fail to allow for the capabilities of the children? Is equipment designed to permit progression dictated by growth and development? Another question that needs to be asked is, "How much rough housing exists in these accidents?"

Risk Management

Playground risk management is the identification, evaluation, and control of loss to the users of the playground. Users of playgrounds are usually thought of as children residing in the area or the public in general. A systematic analysis of the entire play area with an emphasis on exposure to loss and potential liability should be conducted. The results of the research on litigation and accidents discussed above is to be used as one aspect of the determination of potential liability.

Playground supervisors and directors need to be aware that anyone can be sued, a lawsuit is filed when one believes that they have been wronged and that another is responsible for that wrong (see Figure 8.2). Resources to support rehabilitation of the injured party is typi-

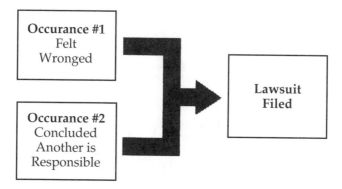

Figure 8.2 A legal action is usually based on two occurrences which take place prior to filing the suit.

cally the reason for suit. Serious injuries tend to result in large medical bills; bills beyond what parents can afford. To finance the child's medical expenses and rehabilitation, the parents find it necessary to request that the court identify the party responsible for the child's injury and cause that party to pay for the damages.

Identification

All areas in which a participant could be exposed to risk should be identified. Playground risks are easily placed into the following categories: facilities, equipment, and supervision.

Facilities

1. *Location of facility*. Many children are injured on their way to and from a playground. Children are injured by trains when railroad right-of-ways are close to playgrounds and by cars when play area entrances and exits are adjacent to busy streets.

2. *Construction of facility*. The placement and location of each piece of equipment and designated play area within the facility should be evaluated with reference to safety.

a. Traffic patterns for movement of children from one piece of equipment to another need to be predicted. Adequate space must be provided for children to exit a piece of equipment rapidly so another child can use the equipment. The validity of the original prediction, made by the planner of the facility, needs to be examined often during prime time use. If the predicted pattern does not appear safe, changes should be made. Manufacturer's recommendations for traffic flow should be consulted as should other sources on the subject.

b. Space should be adequate for the game or sport designated for the area and should be separated from playground equipment. Age groups should also be separated so that a six or seven year old is not found wandering through a league game.

c. The selection of the topical surface and the underpinning beneath the surface may play a major role in future litigation. Considerable attention needs to be devoted to selection of a safe surface. The condition of the surface beneath equipment, abutments with fences and with grass need to be within prescribed guidelines. The U.S. Consumer Product Safety Commission has specified recommendations for surfaces.

3. *Maintenance of the facility*. Design a checklist for the routine safety inspection of the facility. The frequency of the inspection and the name of the inspector should be recorded. If the checklist is used on a weekly basis it should be filled out and signed each week. In addition, a casual walk around should occur each day and more often, if needed.

a. Facilities should be routinely inspected for cleanliness as well as safety. Three playground checklists are available from AAHPERD:

daily, monthly, and a parents' checklist.

b. Broken bottles, glass, and other hazardous materials should be reported at once with participants instructed to vacate the area at first observation of such dangers.

Equipment

1. *Knowledge of Playground Injuries.* Managers of playgrounds should become familiar with national injury statistics on the products (equipment) in use on their specific playground and on playgrounds in general. With falls the number one source of injury, a hard look should be given not only at equipment which is known to cause children to lose their grip or balance, but to equipment similar in nature which has not been on the market sufficiently long to have a track record.

2. *Care of Equipment.* A system should be devised for early detection of broken and defective equipment. It should also include a method of closing equipment in need of repair, providing for repair, and bringing repaired equipment back into use. Equipment should be cleaned on a periodic basis.

3. *Manufacturer's Specifications.* Equipment, accompanied by manufacturer's warranties, must be installed, used, and repaired exactly as stated in the warranty or the warranty is invalidated. The warranty is invalidated if the equipment is repaired by someone other than a designated professional. Manufacturer's recommendations, even if not part of the warranty, should be followed. If the manufacturer does not provide specifications for repair and/or use, the equipment should be maintained and used according to practices within the industry.

4. *Posting of Manufacturer's Warnings and Instructions.* Equipment manufacturer's instructions and warnings should be posted in a conspicuous place. Participants must be able to read and understand manufacturer's printed materials. When necessary the instructions should be translated into Spanish or any other language native to the neighborhood.

5. *Additional information.* For further information on product liability and the professional refer to Wittenburg (1986, 1987) or Clement (1988, Chapter seven).

Supervision

Supervision may or may not exist on a particular playground. Consideration should be given to the provision of signage which will clearly state the existence or nonexistence of supervision and/or the specific times in which supervision exists. When supervision exists as a team coach or a playground supervisor, for example, the exact role of that authority figure must be known to the authority figure, to the playground participants, and to the public in general.

1. *Eliminate all horse play.* Remove children "acting out" from the playground. Penalties need to be established that will punish those

behaving in an unsafe manner to deter them from continuing the behavior (this assumes supervision).

2. *Code of Play*. Establish a behavior code and impress upon children and their parents the need to honor the code.

3. *Self Reporting*. Provide for the reporting of splinters, protruding or missing screws, and jagged edges by participants and personnel. Repair at once or take out of use.

4. *Accidents Reports*. Provide for the routine reporting of accidents and for notification of authorities. These systems need to be tailored to the playground and require planning within the agency. Injured children on playgrounds may represent the child who lives across the street and whose mother works at the local grocery store, or the young unconscious child with no identification who needs immediate medical attention. Provision should also be made for an injury tracking system which notes the details of serious injuries and the frequency of not so serious injuries.

5. *First Aid*. Where supervision exists, a system of immediate and temporary care and a method of obtaining emergency assistance should be created, learned by personnel, and used. If no supervision is present, a telephone with full emergency information should be available.

6. *Governance*. Know state and local statutes pertaining to playgrounds.

Evaluation

All risks or potential for injuries are identified and evaluated to ascertain the extent of the risk or potential for injury involved. Each piece of equipment will, for example, be given a risk assessment. The use of certain equipment will be determined to have a low probability of incurring substantial liability; the use of other equipment will suggest a high level of vulnerability to liability. "Vulnerability is assessed in terms of

1. Probability:
   a. high probability of injury or harm, or
   b. low probability of injury or harm.
2. Severity:
   a. serious injury or death, or
   b. minor discomfort.
3. Magnitude:
   a. many people injured or harmed, or
   b. few people injured or harmed (Clement, 1988, p. 184).

Playground slides, and baseball play and batting, according to the litigation survey, and falls, according to the U.S. Consumer Product Safety Commission, provide a high level of vulnerability.

Control

Once the level of vulnerability for the facility is determined, and each piece of equipment, supervision of the participants, and immediate and temporary care are assessed, the element of control is introduced. In control, a decision is made to eliminate the risk, accept the risk, transfer the risk, or change the activity to reduce potential injury and risk (see Figure 8.3).

When the equipment or activity has little value for the attainment of skill or the acquisition of the child's risk-taking capacity, and at the same time presents a high vulnerability to accident and liability, the equipment or activity should be eliminated. When the activity has a high level of value to the attainment of skill and the acquisition of risk-taking capacity and a high level of vulnerability to potential injury, the two factors must be balanced and a decision made to continue or eliminate the activity. Often the balancing process results in the finding of ways to modify or decrease the vulnerability of the activity. When modification is impossible or inappropriate the activity may be retained in spite of the risk. In this situation, insurance can be incorporated in the risk management plan to reduce the probability of financial loss.

Activities and/or playground equipment essential to the physical growth, risk-taking acquisition, or social interaction of children cannot be removed or eliminated merely because they may be vulnerable to serious accidents which could result in litigation. They can and should be removed, however, when other activities, not so vulnerable to litigation, provide the same physical, risk-taking, and social skills.

Professionals should be aware that playground situations can be made so void of exciting risk-taking opportunities that young people will no longer choose the location for activity and will seek out street corners for their acquisition of physical skills, risk-taking, and socialization. Young children can become so pampered with equipment that is easy to use and eliminates the possibility of falling that the opportunity to acquire arm and shoulder strength no longer exists.

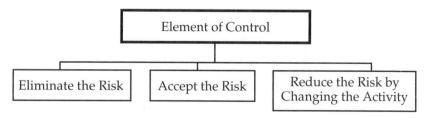

Figure 8.3. An element of control over risk can be gained by using any of these three possible decision sets.

In general, playground personnel should:
• Provide facilities and equipment that are as safe as possible and meet the growth and development needs of physical skill acquisition, risk-taking, and socialization.
• Note that facility and equipment, if supervised, needs to be fully supervised. If not supervised, participants, parents, and the public in general should be aware that the playground is not supervised.

Each employee should also acquire knowledge of:
• Legal rights and responsibilities,
• Results of consumer product safety research,
• Equipment and activities that tend to result most often in injuries,
• Manufacturer's warranties and how they are to be handled,
• Risk management evaluation vulnerability standards in terms of probability, severity, and magnitude.

They should apply this knowledge by:
• Establishing a minimal standard of care,
• Establishing a standard of care to which the agency strives,
• Recognizing the difference between these standards of care,
• Creating and carrying out a risk management program,
• Devising a system for documenting that the standard of care has been maintained,
• Eliminating "horseplay" and "rough house" activity.

The author believes that conscientious playground personnel are currently executing most of the above recommendations. The area most often neglected is documentation. Thus, the greatest need for change is in the creation of a system for documentation. Documentation is vital to prove that you are doing a good job.

Professionals must recognize that anyone can be sued. Most law suits are filed in an effort to identify the party responsible for an injury in which the victim will require substantial resources for rehabilitation. Professionals who have clearly established a standard of care, maintained that standard, provided documentation that the standard was maintained, and obtained council capable of presenting their case should succeed in a court of law. Incompetent and sloppy playground personnel and administrators should be threatened by the thought of litigation; on the other hand, competent personnel and administrators should assume that they will succeed, if challenged in a court of law.

Bibliography

Black, Henry Campbell (1979). *Black's law dictionary, 5th Ed.* St. Paul, MN: West Publishing Company.

Bruya, L. & Beckwith, J. (1988). A System to Manage the Risk of Lawsuit. In L. D. Bruya (ed.), *Play Spaces For Children, Vol. 2.* Reston, VA: AAHPERD.

Clement, Annie (1988). *Law in sport and physical activity*. Indianapolis, IN: Benchmark Press.

Clement, Annie (1987). A selected checklist of risk management concerns in recreation/sport/exercise programs. *Sport, Park and Recreation Law Reporter, 1(2)*, 32. Canton, OH: Professional Reports Corporation.

Clement, Annie (1086). Preventative law: the risk management audit. *Future focus, 27*, Fall ed. Columbus, OH: Ohio Association for Health, Physical Education and Recreation.

Kaiser, Ronald A. (1986). *Liability and law in recreation, parks and sports*. Englewood Cliffs, NJ: Prentice-Hall.

Keeton, W. Page, Ed. (1984). *Prosser and Keeton on the law of torts*. St. Paul, MN: West Publishing Co.

Riffer, Jeffrey K. (1985). (Update, 1988). *Sports and recreational injuries*. Colorado Springs, CO: Shepard's/McGraw-Hill Book Company.

Rutherford, G. W. (1979). *HIA hazard analysis: injuries associated with public playground equipment*. U.S. Consumer Product Safety Commission, May.

U.S. Consumer Product Safety Commission, (1980a). *A handbook for public playground safety, (Vol. I: General guidelines for new and existing playgrounds)*. Washington, D.C.: U.S. Government Printing Office.

U.S. Consumer Product Safety Commission, (1980b). *A handbook for public playground safety, (Vol. II: Technical guidelines for equipment and surfacing)*. Washington, D.C.: U.S. Government Printing Office.

Wittenberg, Jeffrey D. (1986). (Update 1987). *Product liability: recreation and sport equipment*. New York, NY: Law Journal Seminar Press.

9

Plan of Action:
Reflections and
Recommendations
by Ralph W. Smith

The picture of America's community playgrounds that emerges from the preceding chapters is a disturbing one. Many, if not most, of the community parks surveyed do not offer an appropriate play environment for younger children, fail to provide adequate accommodations for adult supervisors, do not furnish signs to assist users, and exclude many children with disabilities. Moreover, the play structures provided on these playgrounds are dominated by traditional pieces of equipment that offer children limited opportunities for social interaction, creative expression, and fine motor development. Most disturbing of all, however, is the revelation that our nation's playgrounds may simply be too unsafe for use by the people for whom they were built — children.

Reflections on Survey Results

Safety

In 1970, Michael Ellis delivered an indictment of America's playgrounds. He stated that playgrounds generally "are duplicated from site to site in a monotony of stereotyped apparatus. They are essentially static, tubular, safe, predictable, and are often pathetic imitations designed to catch an adult's eye" (Brown & Burger, 1984, p. 600). The results of the present survey demonstrate that at least one aspect of Ellis' analysis is no longer accurate — America's community playgrounds are not safe.

The following are some of the most significant safety problems identified by the survey:

- Twenty-six percent of swing equipment had metal and wood seats;
- Only 11 percent of swing equipment had barriers to protect passers-by, including young children;
- The percentage of sharp edges or protrusions on equipment ranged from 13 percent on climbing equipment to 41 percent on rocking equipment;
- Twenty-seven percent of swing equipment had moving parts that were not in good repair;
- Regarding rocking equipment, 22 percent had missing parts, 17 percent had parts that were not securely fastened, and 37 percent had spring actions that allowed for pinches to occur;
- The percentage of play structures with only grass surfacing underneath ranged from 10 percent for rotating and rocking equipment to 21 percent for climbing equipment;
- Eighteen percent of climbing equipment was higher than nine feet;
- Cushion ground strikes were present at only 17 percent of seesaw equipment, and 57 percent would allow a body to pass underneath while in action;
- Forty-one percent of sand play areas were not clear and free of debris;
- Forty-seven percent of wading pools were not fenced and gated, and 21 percent were not clear and free of debris.

It should be kept in mind that the survey instrument did not take into consideration all factors that might affect the safe use of the play equipment; thus, our nation's playgrounds may be even less safe than they appear. For example, the depth and condition of the surface material was not determined. Sand, the most prevalent material surveyed, is an excellent surface for absorbing the impact of a fall from play equipment; however, to be effective it should be at least 10 inches in depth and must be properly maintained to prevent compacting (Hammer, 1988).

Use By Young Children

The developmental importance of play for young children is well accepted. Piaget (1962), Erickson (1963) and others have documented play's contributions to the cognitive, affective, psychomotor, and social growth of children. America's community playgrounds, however, appear to offer limited appropriate play opportunities to young children. Most urban park users are under five years of age (Wallach,

1988); yet, much of our nation's play equipment is designed for use by school-age children, making it difficult or impossible for younger children to use it safely. One-fourth of the playgrounds surveyed did not provide any play equipment for younger children; moreover, only 43 percent provided separate play areas that would maximize safety and provide for age-appropriate physical and social play opportunities. Sand and water play offer especially important developmental experiences for young children, but only 30 sand areas and 6 wading pools were provided among the 198 community playgrounds surveyed.

Signs

If properly constructed and strategically located, signs could make a significant contribution to America's playgrounds, Instructions for safe and efficient use of equipment, warning signs to alert users to potentially dangerous situations, posting of prohibitions (such as pets), and notification of emergency telephone numbers are but a few of the ways signs could be used to improve playgrounds. At present, however, it appears that few community playgrounds use signs to their advantage. Of the playgrounds surveyed, only 2 percent had signs offering help, 11 percent had signs posting restrictions or limited use, and 13 percent used signs to prohibit animals.

Supervision

Children need opportunities for social interaction and cooperative play away from adult intervention. Nevertheless, the conditions prevalent at many community playgrounds are not conducive to safe use by unsupervised children, particularly younger children. The issue of supervision was not clearly addressed by the present survey, but several items indicate that accommodations for adult supervisors are lacking. As noted above, signs that could assist supervisors in communicating playground rules and proper use of equipment are almost nonexistent. In addition, 25 percent of playgrounds with wading areas provided adult seating. Over 80 percent of the community playgrounds surveyed provided an unobstructed view of the play environment, but less than half provided shaded areas that would offer comfort for adult supervisors.

Accessibility

All children face barriers that occasionally limit or prevent their participation in play activities, but children who have disabilities face more barriers and greater barriers than their nondisabled peers (Kennedy, Austin & Smith, 1987). While they may lessen opportunities for play, barriers in no way reduce the *need* for play opportunities among children with disabilities (Beckwith, 1985; Ellis, 1973). Some of the most obvious barriers that confront children with mobility limitations, particularly those who use wheelchairs, are architectural barriers.

Based upon the present survey, it appears that our nation's community playgrounds offer few architecturally barrier-free play opportunities to children with disabilities. Only 14 percent of the play equipment on playgrounds surveyed was designated for use by a child in a wheelchair, and only 16 percent of the play equipment provided for wheelchair accessibility up to the equipment. The latter is particularly disturbing because a child who uses a wheelchair might be able to transfer onto and use a conventional play structure, *providing* he or she could position the wheelchair adjacent to the equipment. If conventional play equipment is accessible to wheelchair users, opportunities for social interaction between children with disabilities and their nondisabled peers would be greatly enhanced. The potential positive outcomes from such integrated play experiences are many, including appropriate responses to peer aggression, increased social and cognitive skills, and improved communication skills for children with disabilities (Odom, Strain, Karge & Smith, 1986). Moreover, integrated play experiences between children with and without disabilities may, in the long run, have a positive impact upon society's acceptance of people with disabilities (see Figure 9.1).

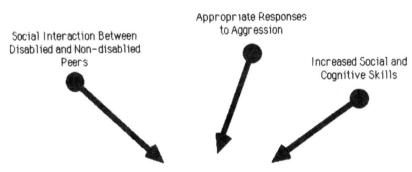

Figure 9.1

Diversity of Experiences

One concept that play theorists generally agree upon is that play environments need to offer a diversity of experiences to children. The variety of children's preferences in playground materials and equipment also supports this concept (Moore, 1974). Playgrounds should enhance arousal seeking behavior by offering a variety of opportunities for exploration, investigation, and manipulation (Ellis, 1973). They should offer a dynamic balance between stability (familiarity) and change (novelty) in order to provide "optimal incongruity" (Iso-Ahola, 1980). Playgrounds and play structures should furnish ample opportunities for individual choice and demonstrations of personal competence (Iso-Ahola, 1980). Furthermore, if playgrounds are to provide an enjoyable experience for children of varying ages and abilities, they need diversity in order to ensure that the "action opportunities" (challenges) offered by play structures are consistent with the "action capabilities" (skills) of children who would seek to use them (Csikszentmihalyi, 1975). Diversity of play experiences is not limited to interaction with facilities and equipment alone, however. The social interaction that takes place among children on playgrounds is an important component of a stimulating and challenging play environment. Conversely, areas that promote quiescence also add to the diversity of a playground.

Diversity, per se, was not examined by the present survey; however, there are some indications that the playgrounds under study lacked sufficient diversity to provide an optimal play environment. For example, the vast majority of the play structures identified in the survey are designed for gross motor activities and encourage aggregate (parallel) or, at best, inter-individual (Avedon, 1974) interaction with the equipment. Structures that could promote greater social interaction and group cooperation were either too narrow to accommodate more than one participant at a time (i.e., slides), or infrequently found on the playgrounds examined. Few of the play structures offered opportunities for fine motor development, nor did they appear to be designed to encourage creative expression and fantasy play. Even the environment surrounding the equipment appears to be inadequate to allow for diversity of play experiences. For example, only 44 percent of the playgrounds surveyed provided hard surfaces for children to ride wheel toys, yet, there is evidence that the presence of such surfaces may be an important variable in the amount of social interaction and locomotor activity exhibited by users of playground (Brown & Burger, 1984).

Recommendations for Change

Assuming that the playgrounds surveyed are representative of America's community playgrounds, it is not surprising that children have been found to go to such traditional playgrounds infrequently, stay for limited periods of time, and rarely consider them their favorite play environments (Hayward, Rothenberg & Beasley, 1974). It is also not surprising that playground-related litigation has been increasing dramatically across the past 30 years. If used as they are designed, most of America's community playgrounds and play structures appear to be both unsafe and boring for children (not to mention inaccessible to children who use wheelchairs). If used by children in creative ways to add novelty and heighten arousal, these play environments might offer stimulation and fun, but they become even more dangerous. No matter how one looks at America's playgrounds, they are desperately in need of change. If implemented, these recommendations should go a long way toward providing community playgrounds that are challenging, stimulating, accessible, and above all, safe for use by our nation's children.

Recommendation 1. Develop a multi-disciplinary approach

The foundation for developing an effective plan of action to change America's playgrounds is accurate and up-to-date information; yet, the professional literature related to play, playgrounds, and their interrelationships is limited and badly fragmented. Leisure and recreation specialists tend to focus upon social-psychological aspects of play; architects and engineers emphasize design and aesthetics; developmental psychologists, physical educators, and other education specialists accentuate physical and psychological development. The results of their research are published in a wide variety of specialized, discipline-related journals, reducing their potential for promoting interdisciplinary understanding. Collaborative efforts are frequent, but they rarely occur between (or among) disciplines that approach the problem from different perspectives. A systematic effort is needed to bring together researchers and theorists, from a variety of academic backgrounds and theoretical perspectives, who are concerned with play and play environments. The focus of this effort should be an integration of our present knowledge about play and play environments in order to provide the foundation for positive change (see Figure 9.2).

Recommendation 2. Form a nationwide task force

If change is to occur on America's playgrounds, a coordinated effort will be needed. A nationwide task force, composed of a cross-section of concerned individuals, could provide the leadership needed to effect change. This task force should be composed of dedicated parents, educators, architects, engineers, legal experts, and profession-

Collaborative Efforts By:

Figure 9.2

als directly concerned with play and play environments. The purpose of the task force would be to develop a comprehensive plan of action for improving our nation's playgrounds and to ensure that the plan is carried out (see Figure 9.3). It is assumed that any plan of action developed by the task force would incorporate some or all aspects of the two recommendations below.

Recommendation 3. Initiate an intensive information and education campaign

Based upon information presently available and the outcomes of a multi-disciplinary effort, a broad-based public information campaign should be initiated. This campaign should focus on a variety of "target populations" in order to develop an understanding of the importance of play and play environments, and promote awareness of the need to improve the safety and play potential of America's playgrounds. Specifically, this campaign should target: (a) the general public—to develop awareness that community playgrounds, as they are presently constructed and maintained, are both unstimulating and unsafe for children; (b) public policy makers and community playground decision makers—to provide them with data emphasizing the benefits

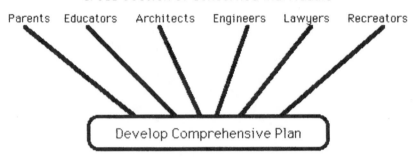

TASK FORCE

Cross Section of Concerned Individuals

Parents   Educators   Architects   Engineers   Lawyers   Recreators

Develop Comprehensive Plan

Figure 9.3

of change versus the costs of inaction; (c) parents and other child supervisors—to stress the importance of play and to provide suggestions for improving both the safety and the developmental potential of playground behavior; and (d) children—to provide "models" for safe and beneficial ways to play on playgrounds (see Figure 9.4).

The following are some suggestions that might be incorporated in a comprehensive information and education campaign:

• Maximize use of the mass media, especially television and newspapers, to publicize the inadequacy of America's community playgrounds. Television efforts could utilize public service advertisements, community information programs, talk shows, and news magazine-type programs (e.g., 60 Minutes) to heighten awareness of unsafe conditions.

• Develop briefing papers and data summaries for distribution to public policy makers. Such documents must be timely and present information that can be put to immediate use; therefore, in order to be effective, these efforts must take place in cooperation with legislative aids;

• Form alliances with consumer-related political action groups, such as Public Citizen, in order to take advantage of their extensive organizations and effective methods;

• Develop a "blue ribbon" speakers bureau to give well-rehearsed presentations at professional conferences, attended by community playground decision makers, such as recreation and park directors, and community planners. Selecting nationally renowned experts and public figures would help ensure attendance at educational sessions and add credibility to both the need for and cost effectiveness of change;

• Produce public service television and radio "spots" specifically

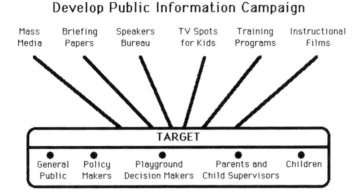

Figure 9.4

targeted to children and designed to promote safe use of playgrounds and playground equipment. Such advertisements should feature a variety of "models" that are salient to young people, and be broadcasted at times of peak viewing (or listening) by children (such as, late afternoons, Saturday mornings).;

• Initiate training programs, including instructional materials, for proper play supervision. These programs should be designed for both parents and playground leaders. As noted by Wallach (1988), "Supervision is a weak link in safety upgrade programs" (p.35);

• Write articles for publication in magazines that are widely read by child caregivers (for example, parent-related magazines). The primary purpose of these articles should be to provide information about the importance of proper adult supervision at play environments. These articles should emphasize safety, but also provide techniques for facilitating play behavior that is both beneficial and fun for the child;

• Develop instructional films and videotapes to assist community playground personnel (for example, leaders and maintenance workers) with identification of safety problems and proper maintenance techniques. Independent efforts, like the Recreation Safety Institutes' hazard identification videotape (Wallach, 1988), should be encouraged.

Recommendation 4. Upgrade/retrofit America's community playgrounds

The number of experts calling for upgrading (or retrofitting) America's playgrounds is increasing (Bruya, 1988; Christiansen, 1987; Lovell & Harms, 1985), and the data from the present survey emphasize this acute need. Moreover, the child-related benefits of improving

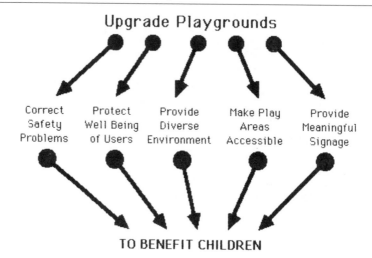

Figure 9.5

playgrounds have been documented (van Andel, 1985; Weinstein & Pinciotti, 1988). Hopefully, the recommendations outlined above will create the broad-based support necessary for this extensive and expensive effort.

Based upon contemporary play theories, humanistic concerns, and safety considerations (see Figure 9.5), upgraded playgrounds must:

• Correct the many safety problems revealed by the present survey. An important step in this effort is to ensure compliance with established safety standards, such as the U.S. Consumer Product Safety Commission's 1982 guidelines (currently under revision) and forthcoming standards from ASTM (American Society for Testing and Materials). In need of *immediate* attention are the surfaces under play equipment, height of play structures, and protective barriers adjacent to swings and other moving structures;

•Protect the psychological, as well as physical, well-being of playground users. Constructing separate play areas for younger children is one way to meet both the physical and psychological needs of users. Another example is offering "face saving" escape routes from some play structures (Simpson, 1988);

• Provide a diverse play environment that is structured to maximize participation and ensure opportunities for social interaction, gross and fine motor development, creative expression, cognitive development, and quiescent activities. Fundamental play concepts, such as optimal arousal (Berlyne, 1960; Ellis, 1973), perceived freedom (Iso-Ahola, 1980), and "flow" (Csikszentmihalyi, 1975), should be considered in the design, development, and modification of play environments. For example, playgrounds should systematically introduce multiple challenges requiring increasingly sophisticated skill levels. They should also provide ample opportunities for exploration, investigation, manipulation, personal choice, and demonstrations of competence;

• Offer adequate accommodations for adult supervisors, including ample seating, good vision of all play areas, and protective shading. The presence of adult supervisors, who intervene only when necessary, also helps to protect both the psychological and physical well-being of playground users.;

• Ensure that some equipment is usable by children in wheelchairs, and provide wheelchair access to most, if not all, pieces of play equipment. Even if a child cannot use a given piece of equipment directly, he or she should not be prevented from being close to the play action (Beckwith, 1985). Because play is so important for children, every effort must be made to ensure that America's playgrounds are accessible to and usable by *all* children who wish to enjoy them. For additional information on making playgrounds accessible to children with disabilities, see Beckwith (1978) and Chapter 5 of Kennedy, et al. (1987);

• Provide signs to assist children and supervisors with proper use of equipment, warn of potential dangers, post prohibition (e.g., pets), and inform playground users of emergency procedures;

• Take into consideration the interactive nature of many aspects of the play environment in order to maximize both safety and participation. Trees, for example, provide shading for users and supervisors, but they also can be seen by children as ecological play structures. Very low, wide trees with an abundance of sturdy limbs might facilitate play, but pruning of all low branches on taller trees is necessary for safety. Poorly maintained pea gravel, a relatively safe surface material, has been demonstrated to limit children's play with vehicular toys (Brown & Burger, 1984) and may constitute a barrier, or even a hazard, for children with mobility limitations.

Indeed, implementation of the above four recommendations, particularly retrofitting and upgrading America's community playgrounds, is a massive undertaking. It will require enormous effort from a large number of dedicated individuals, as well as the expenditure of huge sums of money. However, as Simpson (1988) noted, "Ultimately, each community must determine how much its children are worth as present and future citizens" (p. 63). With so much at stake, can we afford to do less?

Bibliography

Avedon, E. M. (1974). *Therapeutic recreation service: An applied behavioral science approach.* Englewood Cliffs, NJ: Prentice-Hall.

Beckwith, J. (1985). Play environments for all children. *Journal of Physical Education, Recreation and Dance, 20(5),* 10-13. Reston, VA: American Alliance For Health, Physical Education, Recreation, and Dance.

Berlyne, D. E. (1960). *Conflict, arousal and curiosity.* New York: McGraw-Hill.

Brown, J. G., & Burger, C. (1984). Playground designs and preschool children's behaviors. *Environment and Behavior, 16,* 599-626.

Bruya, L. D. (188). The new challenge: Playground upgrades. In L.D. Bruya & S. J. Langendorfer (Eds.) *Where our children play: Elementary school playground equipment.* Reston, VA: American Alliance for Health, Physical Education, Recreation and Dance.

Christiansen, M. L. (1987). It's a jungle gym out there. *Public Risk, 1(3),* 16-17.

Csikszentmihalyi, M. (1975). *Beyond boredom and anxiety.* San Francisco: Jossey-Bass.

Ellis, M. J. (1973). *Why people play.* Englewood Cliffs, NJ: Prentice-Hall.

Erickson, E. H. (1963). *Childhood and society.* (2nd ed.). New York: Norton.

Hammer, N. (1988). How to select a playground surface. *American School and University, 60(7),* 28-29.

Hayward, D. G., Rothenberg, M., & Beasley, R. R. (1974). Children's play and urban playground environments: A comparison of traditional, contemporary and adventure playground types. *Environment and Behavior, 6,* 131-168.

Iso-Ahola, S. E. (1980). *The social psychology of leisure and recreation.* Dubuque, IA: Wm. C. Brown.

Kennedy, D. W., Austin, D. R., & Smith, R. W. (1987). *Special recreation: Opportunities for persons with disabilities.* Philadelphia: Saunders.

Lovell, P. & Harms, T. (1985). How can playgrounds be improved? *Young Children, 40(3),* 3-8.

Moore, R. C. (1974). Anarchy zone: Kids' needs and school yards. *School Review, 82,* 621-645.

Odom, S. L., Strain, P. S., Karger, M. A., & Smith, J. D. (1986). Using single and multiple peers to promote social interaction of preschool children with handicaps. *Journal of the Division of Early Childhood, 10(1),* 53-64.

Piaget, J. (1962). *Play, dreams and imitation in childhood.* London: Norton.

Simpson, N. B. (1988). Playgrounds: Safety and fun by design. *Parks and Recreation, 23(10),* 29-32, 63.

van Andel, J. (1988). Effects of the redevelopment of an elementary school playground. *Leisure Studies, 4*, 307-320.

Wallach, F. (1988). Are we teaching playground abuse? *Parks and Recreation, 23(10)*, 34-36.

Weinstein, C. S., & Pinciotti, P. (1988). Changing a schoolyard: Intentions, design decisions, and behavioral outcomes. *Environment and Behavior, 20*, 345-371.

APPENDICES

APPENDIX A
Mission Statement for the
Committee on Play

AALR-AAHPERD-COP
COMMITTEE ON PLAY

MISSION STATEMENT

• MISSION STATEMENT FOR THE AALAR COMMITTEE ON PLAY

The purposes of the AALR Committee on Play are:

- to understand the nature and function of play

- to support play

- to share information on play

- to educate for play with a focus on the individual, society and setting.

APPENDIX B
Trained Volunteer Survey Administrators

National Community Park Playground Equipment Survey

TRAINED VOLUNTEERS

Sincere appreciation is extended to those professionals who conducted the playground equipment survey in community parks through the United States.

Hezi Aharoni
Columbus, OH

Jimmy Allen
Gastonia, NC

Molly Arthur
Berea, OH

Viola Bahls
Lincoln, NE

D. L. Barber
Pasadena, CA

Louis Bowers
Tampa, FL

Judy Burnett
Bradenton, FL

Joy Callahan
Lincoln, NE

Sheila Caskey
Cape Giardeau, MO

Janet Chartier
Paonia, CO

Trey Crawford
Zephyrhills, FL

Trish Cruea
New Port Richey, FL

Jerry Cunningham
Pinellas Park, FL

Susan Decidue
S. St. Petersburg, FL

Peter Eagleson
Tampa, FL

Patricia Fehl
Morgantown, WV

Thomas Fisher
Berea, KY

Gerard Greer
St. Petersburg, FL

Delmar Harris
Concordia, KS

Larry Isacs
Daytona, OH

R. Melvin Johnson
Richland, MO

Dorothy Kilpatrick
Richmond, KY

Debra Lacy
East Wenatchee, WA

Stephen Langendorfer
Kent, OH

Dorothy Lemieux
Dayton, OH

Sherri Mach
Lawrence, KS

Emily Malcolm
St. Petersburg, FL

Stella Maunsell
Chapel Hill, NC

Jerri McCoy
Charlottesville, VA

Judy Meagley
Ormond Beach, FL

Janice Olson
West Lafayette, IN

Ed Refrow
Siloam Springs, AR

Rick Rizzo
Clearwater, FL

Donna Thompson
Cedar Falls, IA

Carol Torrey
New Orleans, LA

Bob Watson
Madiera Beach, FL

Marsha Watts
Aurora, CO

Sue Wortham
San Antonio, TX

Loyce Willett
Oklahoma City, OK

APPENDIX C
Playground Selection Process

National Survey of Playground Equipment for Parks

Playground Selection Process

AALR-AAHPERD-COP
(COMMITTEE ON PLAY)

1. Acquire a list of all parks in the park district offices for the district you have chosen.

2. Number all parks listed starting with #1.

3. Select the parks you will assess, based on "Park Playground Selection Process" listed below.

Park Playgrond Selection Process
(Used to Pick the Parks to be Assessed)

A. 0-10 parks in district: assess 1 park
#2

B. 10-20 parks in district: assess 2 parks
#2, #18

C. 20-40 parks in district: assess 4 parks
#2, #18, #8, #17

D. 40-70 parks in district: assess 7 parks
#2, #18, #8, #17, #41, #13, #36

E. 70-100 parks in district: assess 10 parks
#2, #18, #8, #17, #41, #13, #36, #94, #26, #81

F. 100-150 parks in district: assess 15 parks
#2, #18, #8, #17, #41, #13, #36, #94, #26, #81, #97, #143, #111, #113, #124

G. 150-200 parks in district; assess 20 parks
#2, #18, #8, #17, #41, #13, #36, #94, #26, #81, #97, #143, #111, #113, #124, #125, #11, #152, #4, #112

H. 200-250 parks in district: assess 25 parks
#2, #18, #8, #17, #41, #13, #36, #94, #26, #81, #97, #143, #111, #113, #124, #125, #11, #152, #4, #112, #212, #131, #230, #25, #70

I. 250-300 parks in district: assess 30 parks
#2, #18, #8, #17, #41, #13, #36, #94, #26, #81, #97, #143, #111, #113, #124, #125, #11, #152, #4, #112, #212, #131, #230, #25, #70, #245, #220, #115, #107, #281

J. 300-350 parks in district: assess *35* parks
#2, #18, #8, #17, #41, #13, #36, #94, #26, #81, #97, #143, #111, #113, #124, #125, #11, #152, #4, #112, #212, #131, #230, #25, #70, #245, #220, #115, #107, #281, #309, #59, #176, #54, #160

K. 350-400 parks in district: assess *40* parks
#2, #18, #8, #17, #41, #13, #36, #94, #26, #81, #97, #143, #111, #113, #124, #125, #11, #152, #4, #112, #212, #131, #230, #25, #70, #245, #220, #115, #107, #281, #309, #59, #176, #54, #160, #351, #382, #282, #153, #114

L. 400-500 parks in district: assess *50* parks
#2, #18, #8, #17, #41, #13, #36, #94, #26, #81, #97, #143, #111, #113, #124, #125, #11, #152, #4, #112, #212, #131, #230, #25, #70, #245, #220, #115, #107, #281, #309, #59, #176, #54, #160, #351, #382, #282, #153, #114, #20, #257, #203, #423, #426, #396, #201, #354, #485, #172

Note: For park districts larger than 500 call L. Bruya collect at 817/ 565-2651, leaving your name, phone and the number of parks in the district. He will return your call with additional numbers of parks to assess.

Please assess each park listed on the list even if it has no play structure. If a park has no play structure, note it on the *National Survey of Playground Equipment For Parks* and send it in.

Please list the # of the park selected on the assessment instrument as well as the number of parks in the district.

APPENDIX D
National Park Playground
Equipment Survey
Instrument Used in the Study

NATIONAL SURVEY OF PLAYGROUND
EQUIPMENT FOR PARKS

April 1986

Name of Person	Date
Conducting Survey	

Beginning Time	Completion Time	Name and Address of the Park

Use the following symbols throughout the survey: ✓ = Yes   X = No

Section 1: Location and Accessibility of Playground Equipment

_____ 1.1 Is the play equipment easily in view of nearby residents and/or passersby?

_____ 1.2 Is there a fence or wall at least 3 feet high surrounding the play equipment?

_____ 1.3 Is access up to the play equipment possible for children in wheelchairs by means of a hard surface?

_____ 1.4 Can wheelchairs get up on any of the play equipment?

Section 2: Placement and Size of Equipment

_____ 2.1 Is there at least 10 feet of space between each piece of equipment and and other structures, so as to avoid collision of moving children?

_____ 2.2 Is all equipment placed so as to avoid collision or interference with traffic patterns of children walking or on wheel toys on designated pathways?

_____ 2.3 Is smaller sized play equipment intended for young children present?

_____ 2.4 If so, is smaller equipment separated from larger equipment by physical distance or a fence or hedge so as to discourage cross over use?

_____ 2.5 Are any concrete footings of inground support structures exposed?

_____2.6 If yes then how many are exposed?

Section 3: Type and Numbers of Equipment

_____3.1 List the numbers of each type of equipment located on school playground:

_____Flat Slides   _____Firemans Poles

_____Tube Slides   _____Monkey Bars

_____Swing Structures   _____Parallel Bars

_____Exer-Glides   _____Overhead Ladders

_____Merry-Go-Round   _____Chinning Bars

_____Seesaws   _____Sand Play Containers

_____Suspended Bridge   _____Water Play Containers

_____Balance Beams   _____Interconnected Play Structures

_____Spring Rockers   _____List Other Equipment:

_____Geodesic Dome Climbers

Section 4: Swinging Equipment

_____4.1 Number of swing seats?

_____4.2 Are any of the swing seats made of metal or wood?

_____4.3 If yes how many?

_____4.4 How many of the swings are of the swivel type?

_____4.5 Are sings designed to accommodate young children present?

_____4.6 Are the swings for younger children on a separate lower structure from the other taller swings?

_____4.7 Have barriers such as a fence or hedge been provided to discourage children from running into swings while swings are in motion?

_____4.8 Are all support structures for the swings firmly anchored in the ground?

_____4.9 Are there any sharp corners, edges, or projections on any part of the swing seat, chains, or swing structure?

___4.10 Are all moving parts in good working condition and not in danger of breaking?

___4.11 Are chains covered to avoid pinch points?

___4.12 What is the shortest distance between each of the swing seats? (measure from outer edge of swing seat to outer edge of the next swing seat)

___4.13 Which of the following surface materials is found under the swings?

____concrete	____clay	____pea gravel
____asphalt	____sand	____rubber matting
____grass	____mulch	____other

_____ If surface material is sand, mulch, or pea gravel how deep is it?

Section 5: Sliding Equipment

_____5.1 Are parts of the equipment broken or not present?

_____5.2 Are there any sharp corners, edges or projections?

_____5.3 Is the supporting structure firmly fixed in the ground?

_____5.4 Is the slide wide enough to accommodate more than one child at the same time?

_____5.5 Is the sliding surface stable, smooth, and with no protrusions throughout its length?

_____5.6 Does the angle of the slide level off at the bottom to cause deceleration before the child reaches the end of the slide?

_____5.7 How high is the end of the slide above ground level?

_____5.8 How many feet from the ground is the standing platform of the slide at its' highest point?

_____5.9 Is there a guardrail around the standing platform area?

_____5.10 Which of the following surface materials is found under the slide?

    _____concrete   _____clay   _____pea gravel

    _____asphalt   _____sand   _____rubber matting

    _____grass   _____mulch   _____other

_____ If surface material is sand, mulch, or pea gravel how deep is it?

Section 6: Climbing Equipment

_____6.1 Are all parts of the equipment securely fastened?

_____6.2 Are structural supports firmly fixed into the ground?

_____6.3 Are there any open holes which form finger traps at the end of the tubes or pipes?

_____6.4 What is the largest diameter of the hand holds needed for climbing?

_____6.5 Are there any sharp corners, edges, or projections?

_____6.6 What is the farthest distance between horizontal levels used for climbing?

_____6.7 Are there any V angles less than 7 inches wide at the base on any part of the equipment likely to cause limbs, feet, or clothing to be trapped?

_____6.8 What is the maximum height from the ground including projections to any platforms that a child can climb to?

_____6.9 Which of the following surface materials is found under the climbing equipment?

    _____concrete   _____clay   _____pea gravel

    _____asphalt   _____sand   _____rubber matting

    _____grass   _____mulch   _____other

_____ If surface material is sand, mulch, or pea gravel how deep is it?

Section 7: Rotating Equipment (Merry-Go-Rounds, Swinging Gates)

____7.1 Is the supporting structure firmly fixed in the ground?

____7.2 Are all joints and fasteners secure?

____7.3 Are there any sharp corners, edges, or projections?

____7.4 Is the area surrounding the rotation post open?

____7.5 Does the minimum perimeter cleared of obstacles extend beyond the equipment 20 feet so as to allow running space coming off of the merry-go-round?

____7.6 Which of the following surface materials is found under the rotating equipment?

____concrete   ____clay   ____pea gravel

____asphalt   ____sand   ____rubber matting

____grass   ____mulch   ____other

____7.7 If the surface material is sand, mulch, or pea gravel how deep is it?

Section 8: Spring Rocking Equipment

____8.1 Are all of the structural supports firmly fixed in the ground?

____8.2 Are all parts of the equipment present?

____8.3 Are all joints and fastenings secure?

____8.4 Are there any sharp corners, edges, or projections?

____8.5 How high from the ground are the seating surfaces?

____8.6 How long is the shorter of the two handholds on the rocking equipment?

____8.7 How wide and how long are the footrests?

____8.8 If there is spring action, can the fingers or toes be pinched?

____8.9 Which of the following surface materials is found under the rocking equipment?

____concrete   ____clay   ____pea gravel

____asphalt   ____sand   ____rubber matting

____grass   ____mulch   ____other

_____ If the surface is sand, mulch, or pea gravel how deep is it?

Section 9: See Saw Equipment

____9.1 Are all of the structural supports firmly fixed in the ground?

____9.2 Are all joints and fastenings secure?

____9.3 Are there any sharp corners, edges, or projections?

____9.4 What is the height of the seating surface when it's at its' highest point?

____9.5 Are there handholds for two hands on each end?

____9.6 Can any part of the body pass beneath the equipment while it is in action so as to be struck?

____9.7 Has any provision been made on the apparatus to cushion its' impact upon striking the ground?

____9.8 Are any of the pivotal moving parts accessible to fingers which might be hurt?

____9.9 Which of the following surface materials is found under rocking equipment?

____concrete   ____clay   ____pea gravel

____asphalt   ____sand   ____rubber matting

____grass   ____mulch   ____other

_____ If the surface material is sand, mulch, or pea gravel how deep is it?

Section 10: Designated Sand Play Area — Sand is Contained Within Area for Digging, etc.

___ 10.1 Is the sand clean and free of debris?

___ 10.2 Does the sand drain freely after rain?

___ 10.3 Is the sand play area elevated or covered to exclude animals digging in it?

___ 10.4 Is there seating for adults provided adjacent to the sand play area?

Section 11: Wading Pools

___ 11.1 Is the pool area fenced and gated to exclude animals?

___ 11.2 Is the water clear and free from debris?

___ 11.3 How many inches is the water measured at the deepest point when the pool is filled?

___ 11.4 Is there adult seating provided adjacent to the wading pool?

Section 12: Signs, Trees, Pathways

___ 12.1 Are there any signs giving details of where to seek help in case of an accident?

___ 12.2 Are there any signs listing any restrictions or limitations in the use of the equipment?

___ 12.3 Are there any sings excluding animals from the playground?

___ 12.4 How many trees are located within a 50 foot area of the placement of the playground equipment?

___ 12.5 Are there any structures which provide shade in addition to trees?

___ 12.6 Are there any hard surfaces for wheel toys?

Return completed Survey to: Dr. Louis Bowers
                             Physical Education Department
                             University of South Florida
                             Tampa, Florida 33620